# OPPOSING VIEWPOINTS® SERIES

# Cyber Crime

MAY

2009

CO

# Other Books of Related Interest:

## Opposing Viewpoints Series

Criminal Justice

Technology and Society

## At Issue Series

Has Technology Increased Learning?

What Is the Impact of Cyberlife?

## Current Controversies Series

Blogs

Online Social Networking

"Congress shall make
no law . . . abridging
the freedom of speech,
or of the press."

*First Amendment to the U.S. Constitution*

The basic foundation of our democracy is the First Amendment guarantee of freedom of expression. The Opposing Viewpoints Series is dedicated to the concept of this basic freedom and the idea that it is more important to practice it than to enshrine it.

# OPPOSING VIEWPOINTS® SERIES

# Cyber Crime

*Louise I. Gerdes, Book Editor*

**GREENHAVEN PRESS**
*A part of Gale, Cengage Learning*

GALE
CENGAGE Learning™

Detroit • New York • San Francisco • New Haven, Conn • Waterville, Maine • London

Christine Nasso, *Publisher*
Elizabeth Des Chenes, *Managing Editor*

© 2009 Greenhaven Press, a part of Gale, Cengage Learning.

Gale and Greenhaven Press are registered trademarks used herein under license.

*For more information, contact:*
Greenhaven Press
27500 Drake Rd.
Farmington Hills, MI 48331-3535
Or you can visit our Internet site at gale.cengage.com

For product information and technology assistance, contact us at

Gale Customer Support, 1-800-877-4253
For permission to use material from this text or product, submit all requests online at
www.cengage.com/permissions

Further permissions questions can be emailed to permissionrequest@cengage.com

Articles in Greenhaven Press anthologies are often edited for length to meet page requirements. In addition, original titles of these works are changed to clearly present the main thesis and to explicitly indicate the author's opinion. Every effort is made to ensure that Greenhaven Press accurately reflects the original intent of the authors. Every effort has been made to trace the owners of copyrighted material.

Cover photograph reproduced by permission of Stockbyte/PunchStock.

**LIBRARY OF CONGRESS CATALOGING-IN-PUBLICATION DATA**

Cyber crime / Louise I. Gerdes, book editor.
   p. cm. -- (Opposing viewpoints)
  Includes bibliographical references and index.
  ISBN-13: 978-0-7377-4200-8 (hardcover)
  ISBN-13: 978-0-7377-4201-5 (pbk.)
  1. Computer crimes. I. Gerdes, Louise I., 1953-
  HV6773.C913 2009
  364.16'8--dc22

                                             2008027519

Printed in the United States of America
1 2 3 4 5 6 7 12 11 10 09 08

# Contents

Why Consider Opposing Viewpoints?     **11**

Introduction     **14**

## Chapter 1: Is Cyber Crime a Serious Problem?

Chapter Preface     **19**

1. Identity Theft Is a Serious Problem     **21**
   *Chris Swecker*

2. Identity Theft Is a Declining Problem     **26**
   *Thomas M. Lenard*

3. Cyber-Terrorism Poses a Serious Threat
   to Global Security     **35**
   *Simon Finch*

4. The Problem of Cyberterrorism
   Is Exaggerated     **40**
   *Joshua Green*

5. Internet Piracy Threatens the
   Entertainment Industry     **51**
   *Orrin Hatch*

6. The Problem of Internet Piracy Is Overstated     **57**
   *Dave McClure*

7. Online Predators Are a Serious Threat     **62**
   *Jeff Buckstein*

8. The Media Stereotype of Online Predators
   Is Inaccurate     **68**
   *Janis Wolak, David Finkelhor, Kimberly J. Mitchell,
   and Michele L. Ybarra*

Periodical Bibliography     **77**

# Chapter 2: What Factors Contribute to Cyber Crime?

Chapter Preface    **79**

1. Organizational Mismanagement, Not Hackers,    **81**
   Explain Most Data Breaches
   *Frank Washkuch Jr.*

2. Vigilantism Motivates Some to Violate Cyber Laws    **86**
   *Nancy Gohring*

3. Peer-to-Peer File-Sharing Is a Form of Rebellion    **91**
   Against Corporate Tyranny
   *Marc Freedman*

4. The Internet Helps Promote Terrorism    **95**
   *Steve Coll and Susan B. Glasser*

5. Stalkers Use the Internet to Pursue Their Victims    **104**
   *Kacy Silverstein*

Periodical Bibliography    **110**

# Chapter 3: How Can Companies and Consumers Reduce the Impact of Cyber Crime?

Chapter Preface    **112**

1. Consumers Should Be Allowed to Freeze    **114**
   Their Credit History
   *Anita Ramasastry*

2. Consumers Should Not Be Allowed    **120**
   to Freeze Their Credit History
   *Stuart Pratt*

3. Software Manufacturers Should Be Liable    **123**
   for Internet Security Breaches
   *Bruce Schneier*

4. Software Companies Should Not Be Liable     **127**
for Internet Security Breaches
*Harris Miller*

5. Colleges Should Play a Greater Role in     **131**
Combating Internet Piracy
*Graham Spanier*

6. Combating Internet Piracy Is Not an Appropriate     **135**
Role for Colleges
*Mark Luker and Michael Petricone*

Periodical Bibliography     **140**

## Chapter 4: What Laws Will Best Prevent Cyber Crime?

Chapter Preface     **142**

1. A Federal Data Breach Notification Standard     **144**
Is Necessary
*William Yurcik and Ragib Hasan*

2. Weak Federal Disclosure Laws Will Not     **150**
Protect Consumers
*Bruce Schneier*

3. The Cybercrime Treaty Will Improve the     **156**
Global Fight Against Internet Crime
*Cyber Security Industry Alliance*

4. The Cybercrime Treaty Threatens Civil Liberties     **162**
*Bob Barr*

5. A Crackdown on Student Internet Copyright     **166**
Infringers Is Necessary
*Mitch Bainwol and Cary Sherman*

6. A Crackdown on Student File-Sharing Is     **173**
an Ineffective Strategy
*Fred von Lohmann*

7. A Federal Cyber-Stalking Law Will
   Protect Victims
   *Jim McDermott*                                    **177**

8. The Federal Cyber-Stalking Law Violates
   Free Speech
   *Wendy McElroy*                                    **182**

Periodical Bibliography                               **188**
For Further Discussion                                **189**
Organizations to Contact                              **192**
Bibliography of Books                                 **199**
Index                                                 **202**

# Why Consider Opposing Viewpoints?

> *"The only way in which a human being can make some approach to knowing the whole of a subject is by hearing what can be said about it by persons of every variety of opinion and studying all modes in which it can be looked at by every character of mind. No wise man ever acquired his wisdom in any mode but this."*
>
> *John Stuart Mill*

In our media-intensive culture, it is not difficult to find differing opinions. Thousands of newspapers and magazines and dozens of radio and television talk shows resound with differing points of view. The difficulty lies in deciding which opinion to agree with and which "experts" seem the most credible. The more inundated we become with differing opinions and claims, the more essential it is to hone critical reading and thinking skills to evaluate these ideas. Opposing Viewpoints books address this problem directly by presenting stimulating debates that can be used to enhance and teach these skills. The varied opinions contained in each book examine many different aspects of a single issue. While examining these conveniently edited opposing views, readers can develop critical thinking skills such as the ability to compare and contrast authors' credibility, facts, argumentation styles, use of persuasive techniques, and other stylistic tools. In short, the Opposing Viewpoints Series is an ideal way to attain the higher-level thinking and reading skills so essential in a culture of diverse and contradictory opinions.

In addition to providing a tool for critical thinking, Opposing Viewpoints books challenge readers to question their own strongly held opinions and assumptions. Most people form their opinions on the basis of upbringing, peer pressure, and personal, cultural, or professional bias. By reading carefully balanced opposing views, readers must directly confront new ideas as well as the opinions of those with whom they disagree. This is not to simplistically argue that everyone who reads opposing views will—or should—change his or her opinion. Instead, the series enhances readers' understanding of their own views by encouraging confrontation with opposing ideas. Careful examination of others' views can lead to the readers' understanding of the logical inconsistencies in their own opinions, perspective on why they hold an opinion, and the consideration of the possibility that their opinion requires further evaluation.

## Evaluating Other Opinions

To ensure that this type of examination occurs, Opposing Viewpoints books present all types of opinions. Prominent spokespeople on different sides of each issue as well as well-known professionals from many disciplines challenge the reader. An additional goal of the series is to provide a forum for other, less known, or even unpopular viewpoints. The opinion of an ordinary person who has had to make the decision to cut off life support from a terminally ill relative, for example, may be just as valuable and provide just as much insight as a medical ethicist's professional opinion. The editors have two additional purposes in including these less known views. One, the editors encourage readers to respect others' opinions—even when not enhanced by professional credibility. It is only by reading or listening to and objectively evaluating others' ideas that one can determine whether they are worthy of consideration. Two, the inclusion of such viewpoints encourages the important critical thinking skill of objectively evaluating an author's credentials and bias. This evaluation will illuminate an author's reasons for taking a particular stance on an issue and will aid in readers' evaluation of the author's ideas.

It is our hope that these books will give readers a deeper understanding of the issues debated and an appreciation of the complexity of even seemingly simple issues when good and honest people disagree. This awareness is particularly important in a democratic society such as ours in which people enter into public debate to determine the common good. Those with whom one disagrees should not be regarded as enemies but rather as people whose views deserve careful examination and may shed light on one's own.

Thomas Jefferson once said that "difference of opinion leads to inquiry, and inquiry to truth." Jefferson, a broadly educated man, argued that "if a nation expects to be ignorant and free . . . it expects what never was and never will be." As individuals and as a nation, it is imperative that we consider the opinions of others and examine them with skill and discernment. The Opposing Viewpoints Series is intended to help readers achieve this goal.

*David L. Bender and Bruno Leone,*
*Founders*

# Introduction

*"Though e-commerce and e-government are growing steadily, industry analysts and government officials wonder how much more would be possible, were it not for persistent consumer concerns about the privacy of 'doing business' on the Internet—the world's most public marketplace."*

—*Cindy J. Lackey,*
*Senior Policy Analyst*
*at The Council of State Governments.*

The nature and scope of the Internet has changed since it was developed in the 1960s. The Internet was first created to maintain communications in the event of nuclear war. Traditional communication networks, such as the telephone system, route information through central switching points that if attacked, would prevent the delivery of vital communications. To avoid this problem, military researchers proposed a communication network that would send small "packets" of digitized information to their destination on a network with many nodes. According to science fiction writer Bruce Sterling, each digital packet "would be tossed like a hot potato from node to node to node, more or less in the direction of its destination, until it ended up in the proper place. If big pieces of the network had been blown away, that simply wouldn't matter; the packets would still stay airborne, lateralled wildly across the field by whatever nodes happened to survive."

The first practical application of this vision was funded by the Defense Department's Advanced Research Projects Agency (DARPA). In 1969, seven large computers at U.S research institutions across the United States were linked to a high-speed, non-centralized packet-switching network called ARPANET. During the 1970s, the number of computer networks linked to ARPANET grew, and by the 1980s, millions of computers—business and personal—were connected to what is now known as the Internet. As the Internet grew, businesses began to recognize its potential. By the late 1990s, e-commerce was quickly expanding, and Web sites became the latest way for businesses to market their products and services.

With the growth in e-commerce, however, came a corresponding growth in e-commerce crime—the most common form of cyber crime. Despite the speed and convenience of e-commerce, fears of cyber crimes such as identity theft and credit-card fraud continue to keep many Americans from banking or shopping online. Those who hope to allay consumer fears and promote the growth of e-commerce claim that e-commerce is as safe as traditional commerce. Consumer advocates, however, assert that e-commerce poses a serious threat to consumers. This debate is in many ways reflective of the overarching cyber crime debate—how best to maintain Internet freedom, speed, and convenience while also protecting privacy and the security of users and consumer information.

Many of those who believe that the unfettered use of the Internet will benefit society also contend that e-commerce is, on the whole, safe. According to Emily Hackett, executive director of the Internet Alliance, "The Internet is a safer place for shopping than the neighborhood mall or downtown department store." In traditional stores, identity thieves can steal carelessly discarded credit-card receipts; unscrupulous retail clerks or restaurant wait staff can also steal patrons' credit-card information. "It takes a sophisticated thief to hack into a Web server," claims Kenneth Kerr, a senior analyst with Gartner, an Internet research company. "It is a lot simpler to steal identity information in a physical environment like a restaurant," he reasons. E-commerce champions emphasize that on the Internet, credit-card transactions are much safer. Hoping to assuage consumer fears, merchants in the online marketplace have invested in sophisticated security technology to protect their e-commerce patrons. "The vast majority of online transactions are carried out without any problems at all," Hackett affirms.

E-commerce advocates suggest that widespread misconceptions about e-commerce crime may account for consumer concern. Contrary to common wisdom, one of the most feared crimes, identity theft, is rarely an online crime. One explanation for consumer confusion, claims Hackett, is that "an identity stolen offline is often used online to defraud a consumer and a marketer." However, she asserts, merchants are working diligently to combat this type of fraud because they are in fact the ultimate victims of credit-card fraud. "The major credit-card companies, by law, never expose the consumer to more than a $50 loss," Hackett maintains. "In fact," she asserts, "VISA and MasterCard guarantee zero liability for consumers." Online merchants are therefore doubly motivated—they hope to allay fears in order to encourage e-commerce and at the same time protect themselves from unnecessary losses. "Online retailers," Hackett reasons, "are working to improve consumer confidence, so the Internet can become the marketplace of the twenty-first century."

Those who believe in the necessity of strict Internet restrictions see e-commerce as more dangerous than traditional commerce. Unwary consumers, they allege, should be better protected from thieves and irresponsible merchants. "Consumers don't trust the Internet. And, they shouldn't," claims Edmund Mierzwinski, consumer program director of the U.S. Public Interest Research Group. "While the notion that hackers might nab your numbers as they hurtle through space is largely false," Mierzwinski maintains, "the problem of hackers or thieving employees breaking into poorly designed Web-merchant computers is real." E-commerce critics contend that many merchants are not doing enough to protect consumers. According to consumer fraud expert Meredith Outwater, "There are merchants who have their [customers'] credit-card data just sitting on servers, waiting to be hacked." Indeed, Outwater argues, "fraud-minded hackers constantly surf the Internet looking for these kinds of opportunities."

Internet crime reports tend to support the claims of e-commerce detractors. According to the 2007 Internet Crime Report, an annual report compiled by the Internet Crime Complaint Center, 2007 losses due to Internet crime reached $240 million, an increase of 25 percent from the previous year. Indeed, many law-enforcement officials admit that they have a difficult time keeping pace with e-commerce fraud. "There's no way that we can police the entire Web with the small staff that we have at this agency," says a Federal Trade Commission (FTC) official. "We go after things that are particularly egregious or pernicious, but we really have to strategically target our limited resources," the official concedes.

Whether e-commerce is safe or dangerous remains hotly contested as is the broader controversy over how best to fight cyber crime while at the same time maintaining the social and economic advantages of an unfettered Internet. The authors of the viewpoints in *Opposing Viewpoints: Cyber Crime* explore these and other issues concerning the nature and scope of Internet crime in the following chapters: Is Cyber Crime a Serious Problem? What Factors Contribute to Cyber Crime? How Can Companies and Consumers Reduce the Impact of Cyber Crime? What Laws Will Best Prevent Cyber Crime?

# CHAPTER 1

# Is Cyber Crime a Serious Problem?

# Chapter Preface

One of the many claimed benefits of the Internet is that it connects people with common interests. Although the Internet was originally developed to allow scientists to conduct research on remote computers, by the early 1970s, e-mail had become the primary form of Internet communication, and much of this e-mail communication was social. Since that time, cyber-socializing applications, such as chat rooms and social-networking sites, have made socializing online much easier, and during the 1990s, the popularity of online social networking grew significantly. While people in chat rooms often use pseudonyms, on social-networking sites users post profiles and photos of themselves, making it easier for other users to discover a lot of information about them. High-profile cases of young girls lured from home and sexually assaulted by men who posed as teens on social-networking sites have heightened fears about the dangers of cyberspace. While some commentators claim that cyberspace is dangerous, other analysts assert that cyber encounters pose no greater risk than real-life encounters.

In the eyes of some, the nature of cyberspace makes it a more dangerous place than real space, especially for children. According to software security expert, John Carosella, "When [inappropriate adult/child communication] happens in real life you know it's happening." The same is not true in cyberspace, he maintains. On the Internet, parents may not know that their children are talking to someone much older. "That is why it can go on with such facility," Carosella contends, "and it's so easy to escalate because nobody can overhear it." Cyberspace can be more dangerous for adults as well. Online communication poses a greater risk than communication in real life, some commentators claim. "Most of our evolutionary clues [to risk] are stripped out" of online encounters, Carosella reasons. The cues people use to assess other people and their motives such as gestures and tone of voice are absent in cyber communication.

For other observers, cyberspace presents no more danger than the real world. According to Northwestern University professor Justine Cassell, "There is no evidence that the online world is more dangerous." In fact, Cassell claims, sex crimes have been steadily decreasing. Even as online socializing grows, she explains, research shows no corresponding increase in sexual predation. The dangers of online and offline dating are about the same, claims Eric Straus, CEO of Cupid.com. Straus asserts that people can be deceived in either environment. "If you talk to 100 people online, some are going to be unsavory," he maintains. "If you meet them in a bar, and they say they're not married, you shouldn't believe that either, and if you give them your phone number, that's dangerous," Straus asserts. Some cyberspace defenders claim that the media have exaggerated the threat that sites such as MySpace pose for teens. According to Danah Boyd, who studies how teens use online technology, "Statistically speaking, kids are more at risk at a church picnic or a Boy Scout outing."

Whether cyberspace is more dangerous than real space remains hotly contested. The authors in the following chapter present their views in answer to the question, is cyber crime a serious problem?

*"Identity theft has emerged as one of the dominant white collar crime problems of the twenty-first century."*

# Identity Theft Is a Serious Problem

*Chris Swecker*

*In the following viewpoint, Chris Swecker argues that identity theft is a persistent and mounting problem. Identity thieves acquire personal information such as Social Security numbers to open new accounts in the victim's name or withdraw funds from existing accounts. Financial institutions suffer because they often bear the costs of the fraudulent use of victim funds, Swecker asserts. He adds that victims suffer because they lose the ability to use their credit. Swecker, former assistant director of the FBI's Criminal Investigative Division, is director for corporate security at Bank of America.*

As you read, consider the following questions:

1. According to Swecker, why does the FBI not track identity theft convictions and indictments?

2. What did a May 2003 Federal Trade Commission survey reveal?

Chris Swecker, "Statement of Chris Swecker, assistant director, Criminal Investigative Division, Federal Bureau of Investigation," Before the Senate Judiciary Committee, April 13, 2005. Reproduced by permission.

3. In the author's opinion, what have breaches of security at large providers of public source data highlighted?

The FBI [Federal Bureau of Investigation] views identity theft as a significant and growing crime problem, especially as it relates to the theft of consumer information from large wholesale data companies. The FBI opened 1,081 investigations related to identity theft in fiscal 2003, and 889 in fiscal 2004. That number is expected to increase as identity thieves become more sophisticated and as the technique is further embraced by large criminal organizations, placing more identity theft crime within FBI investigative priorities. [As of April 2005] the FBI has over 1,600 active investigations involving some aspect of identity theft. These cases are tracked utilizing a crime problem indicator code.

The FBI does not specifically track identity theft convictions and indictments, as identity theft crosses all program lines and is usually perpetrated to facilitate other crimes such as credit card fraud, check fraud, mortgage fraud, and health care fraud.

## The Scope of Identity Theft

Armed with a person's identifying information, an identity thief can open new accounts in the name of a victim, borrow funds in the victim's name, or take over and withdraw funds from existing accounts of the victim, such as their checking account or their home equity line of credit. Although by far the most prevalent, these financial crimes are not the only criminal uses of identity theft information, which can even include evading detection by law enforcement in the commission of violent crimes. Identity theft takes many forms, but generally includes the acquiring of an individual's personal information such as Social Security number, date of birth, mother's maiden name, account numbers, address, etc., for use in criminal activities such as obtaining unauthorized credit and/or bank accounts for fraudulent means.

Identity theft has emerged as one of the dominant white collar crime problems of the twenty-first century. Estimates vary regarding the true impact of the problem, but agreement exists that it is pervasive and growing. In addition to the significant harm caused to the monetary victims of the frauds, often providers of financial, governmental or other services, the individual victim of the identity theft may experience a severe loss in their ability to utilize their credit and their financial identity. This loss can be short in duration, or may extend for years. It may result in the inability to cash checks, obtain credit, purchase a home, or in the most insidious cases, the arrest of the individual for crimes committed by the identity thief.

A May 2003 survey, commissioned by the Federal Trade Commission (FTC) estimated the number of consumer victims of identity theft over the year prior to the survey at 4.6 percent of the population of U.S. consumers over the age of eighteen, or 9.91 million individuals with losses totaling $52.6 billion. However, over half of these victims experienced only the take-over of existing credit cards, which is generally not considered identity theft. New account frauds, more generally considered to be identity theft, were estimated to have victimized 3.23 million consumers and to have resulted in losses of $36.7 billion.

## Developing Joint Initiatives

The FBI's Cyber Division also investigates instances of identity theft which occur over the Internet, or through computer intrusions by hackers.

In recognition of this fact, and the overriding need to gather the most complete and accurate intelligence as quickly as possible, the FBI has focused its efforts on developing joint investigative initiatives with our partners in law enforcement, as well as key Internet e-commerce stake holders. These initiatives have targeted escalating cyber crimes, both domestically

# Common Ways ID Theft Happens

1. *Dumpster Diving.* They rummage through trash looking for bills or other paper with your personal information on it.

2. *Skimming.* They steal credit/debit card numbers by using a special storage device when processing your card.

3. *Phishing.* They pretend to be financial institutions or companies and send spam or pop-up messages to get you to reveal your personal information.

4. *Changing Your Address.* They divert your billing statements to another location by completing a "change of address" form.

5. *"Old-Fashioned" Stealing.* They steal wallets and purses; mail, including bank and credit card statements; pre-approved credit offers; and new checks or tax information. They steal personnel records from their employers, or bribe employees who have access.

*Federal Trade Commission,*
*Fighting Back Against Identity Theft, May 2006.*

and internationally, and invariably included numerous incidents which could be characterized as identity theft.

The Internet Crime Complaint Center, otherwise known as IC3, is a joint project between the FBI and the National White Collar Crime Center. This joint collaboration serves as a vehicle to receive, develop, and refer criminal complaints regarding the rapidly expanding arena of cyber crime. The IC3 receives on average more than 17,000 complaints every month from consumers alone and additionally receives a growing volume of referrals from key e-commerce stakeholders. Of the more than 400,000 complaints referred to the IC3 since its opening in May of 2000, more than 100,000 were either characterized as identity theft, or involved conduct that could be characterized as identity theft.

## A Growing Problem

It should be noted that identity theft in its many forms is a growing problem and is manifested in many ways, including large scale intrusions into third party credit card processors, theft from the mails of printed checks, pre-approved credit card offers and mortgage documents, credit card skimming, phishing schemes, and telephone and bank frauds, much of which is perpetrated through the use of SPAM e-mail.

The FBI is developing cooperative efforts to address the identity theft crime problem. In cities such as Detroit, Chicago, Memphis and Mobile, task forces are currently operating in conjunction with other federal, state and local authorities as well as with affected merchants. In cities such as Tampa, San Diego, and Philadelphia, efforts are underway to create or expand identity theft working groups and task forces. In addition, the FBI is focusing analytical resources on identity theft, working with other agencies, such as the FTC, to obtain identity theft data and utilize it to proactively identify and target organized criminal groups and enterprises.

Computer intrusions, or hackers, can significantly contribute to the impact and scope of identity theft. Breaches of security at large providers of public source data have ... highlighted the ability of criminals to exploit the availability of data.

*"Data on identity theft and its costs . . . do not support the public perception that identity theft is a growing problem."*

# Identity Theft Is a Declining Problem

*Thomas M. Lenard*

*In the following viewpoint, Thomas M. Lenard claims the public perception that identity theft is a mounting problem is mistaken. In fact, he maintains, identity theft is on the decline. Lawmakers should not overreact and enact unnecessary notification rules that reduce innovation and slow growth and productivity, Lenard asserts. He argues that the ready availability of personal information is valuable for both businesses and consumers. Moreover, Lenard reasons, businesses have strong incentives to avoid the unauthorized release of personal information. Lenard is president and senior fellow at iGrowthGlobal and coauthor of* Privacy and the Commercial Use of Personal Information.

Thomas M. Lenard, "Statement of Thomas M. Lenard, Ph.D., senior fellow and senior vice president for research, The Progress & Freedom Foundation, Privacy in the Commercial World II," Before the Subcommittee on Commerce, Trade, and Consumer Protection, Committee on Energy and Commerce, United States House of Representatives, June 20, 2006. Reproduced by permission.

As you read, consider the following questions:

1. In Lenard's opinion, in what area does the United States have a significant advantage over other countries with restrictive data and privacy laws?

2. Why do markets work better with more information, in the author's view?

3. According to the author, why is it not surprising that fraud costs are declining?

The advances in information technology that define the digital revolution have reduced the costs of gathering, storing, manipulating and transmitting information of all kinds. While the economic and social impacts of these advances have been overwhelmingly positive, they also have raised concerns on the part of individuals about what information is being collected, how it is being used, who has access to it, and how secure it is. These concerns have been exacerbated by a series of high-profile data-security breaches that have exposed millions of individuals to potential fraud and convinced much of the public that we face an epidemic of identity theft.

## Evaluating How to Regulate

When considering whether and how to regulate, however, we need to be mindful that we truly do live in an information economy and that the personal information utilized by firms produces great value for consumers and the economy. It is the reason, for example, why any individual with a decent credit rating can get a loan approved virtually instantaneously. It also facilitates competition, generally making it easier for new firms to enter markets that require customer data. It is an area where the United States has a significant advantage over other countries that have more restrictive data and privacy laws and where consumer credit markets and other markets that rely on personal information don't work as smoothly.

Moreover, regulation will inevitably have unpredictable and unintended consequences, especially when imposed on a medium like the Internet that is changing so rapidly. Perhaps the most serious potential cost is a loss of innovation—new uses of information and of the Internet itself that would be frustrated by a new regulatory regime. There are many examples of ways in which information is now being used that were not contemplated when the information was collected, and which would be precluded by some of the measures that have been proposed.

In deciding whether additional regulation is desirable, and, if so, in what form, the following basic public policy questions need to be addressed:

- Are there "failures" in the market for personal information?

- If market failures exist, how do they adversely affect consumers?

- Can such failures be remedied by government action?

- Will the benefits of government regulation exceed the costs?

## The Market for Personal Information

Although privacy and data security are obviously inextricably intertwined, it is useful to think of them separately for the purposes of regulatory analysis. So, the first question is whether there are failures in the market for information and, in particular, whether consumers are being harmed by the *legal use* of personal information for commercial purposes. The answer is that, despite widespread perceptions that personal information is subject to misuse, there does not appear to be much in the way of evidence, even anecdotal evidence, of such harm.

Implicit in the proposals to regulate the market for personal information is that there is a market failure resulting in "too much" information being produced, disseminated and used. As a general matter, however, markets work better with more information. As the cost of information goes down, market participants obtain more of it and, consequently, make better decisions. For example, consumers benefit from receiving information that is better targeted to their interests, as well as from not receiving information that is not of interest to them. Similarly, legitimate marketers have an interest in not sending messages to consumers who aren't interested in them. Merchants with more information can better estimate demand, reducing inventory costs and even lessening swings in overall economic activity. They can also use geographic computer-based information to put their new stores in locations that best serve consumers, and to stock the most useful merchandise for those consumers. . . .

The market also appears to provide incentives for firms to respond to consumers' privacy concerns in a variety of ways. Firms that violate consumer expectations about privacy face a loss of "reputation" that translates into losses in the marketplace. When a firm does something that is perceived as harming its reputation with consumers, the firm suffers a substantial loss in value. Firms, therefore, have a strong incentive to avoid undertaking policies that risk offending their customers. The Internet speeds the collection of information about consumers, but it also enables consumers to more easily obtain information about firms' activities on the Web. In addition, voluntary standards, defined and enforced by third parties or consortia of Web operators, are an important mechanism for providing information to consumers about Web sites' information policies. Finally, new technologies, such as spam filters, are available to consumers who are concerned about privacy.

## The Data Security Question

Data security presents a slightly different issue. While there may be no evidence of market failure or consumer harm from the legal use of personal information in commercial markets,

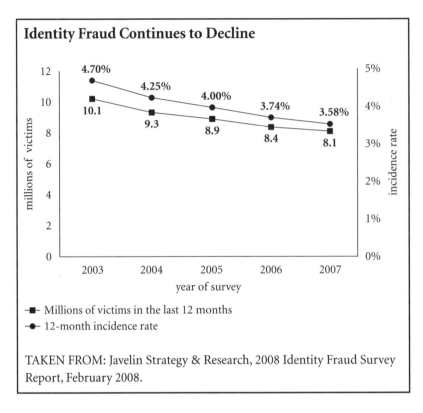

**Identity Fraud Continues to Decline**

TAKEN FROM: Javelin Strategy & Research, 2008 Identity Fraud Survey Report, February 2008.

that does not necessarily imply that firms have the appropriate incentives to safeguard the information under their control or take appropriate steps, whatever these may be, if the data are compromised.

The most recent data on identity theft and its costs (from a 2006 report from Javelin Strategy and Research) do not support the public perception that identity theft is a growing problem. They show that the costs of identity fraud have been essentially constant over the last several years for which data are available (which would indicate that, in a growing economy, they have been declining relative to total transactions). Since 2003, the number of victims of identity fraud has declined by almost 12 percent—to 8.9 million annually—while the average cost per victim has increased by over 20 percent. However, since most victims don't incur the costs related to their fraud cases, the average consumer costs have declined by 24 percent, although the time it takes consumers to resolve fraud cases has increased from 33 to 40 hours.

Other data suggest that costs have been decreasing over time. Estimates by Nilson show that over a longer period—1992 to 2004—the costs of credit card frauds decreased from $0.157 to $0.047 per $100 in credit card sales. Similarly, Visa recently indicated that its fraud costs are at an all-time low of five cents per $100 of transactions. This is a reflection of the fact that credit card firms are continually updating and improving levels of security. The Nilson Report also indicates that fraudulent charges are lower as a percentage of credit card use in the United States than in the rest of the world; for example, credit card payments in the United States are three times the UK level, as compared with fraudulent charges, which are only about 1.2 times the UK level.

It shouldn't be surprising that fraud costs per dollar of transaction are declining. About 90 percent of the costs of identity theft and related frauds are borne directly by businesses, including banks, credit card issuers and merchants. In addition, studies show that firms suffer large losses in stock value when security is breached. Interestingly, these studies are from a period before any consumer notification was required. Despite the perception that information about security breaches was unavailable prior to enactment of the California notification requirement, information about breaches did become public before that time—perhaps as a result of securities regulatory requirements—and markets reacted accordingly. Thus, even without any laws mandating notice to consumers, firms have had a very strong incentive to avoid data security breaches because the market penalizes them severely.

## The Costs of Notification

It is unclear whether firms also have adequate incentives to notify compromised consumers, so the issue is an empirical one: do the benefits of notification outweigh the costs? This issue was addressed in an economic analysis of notification requirements for data security breaches I recently did with Paul Rubin, who is a professor of law and economics at Emory University as well as an adjunct PFF [Progress & Freedom Foundation] fellow.

We found that a notification requirement is dubious on benefit-cost grounds. The expected benefits to consumers of such a requirement are extremely small—probably under $10 per individual whose data have been compromised. There are several reasons for this. First, most cases of identity theft involve offline security breaches, which are not affected by notification requirements. Second, the probability of an individual compromised by a security breach becoming an identity-theft victim is extremely small. Third, most of these are victims of fraudulent charges on their existing credit accounts, for which they have very limited liability, rather than victims of true identity theft. Finally, even a well-designed notification program is likely to eliminate only a small fraction of the expected costs.

While the direct costs of notification may not be large, the indirect costs both to consumers and to sectors of the economy that depend on the free flow of information are likely to be substantial, primarily because of the likelihood that both consumers and firms suffering a security breach will overreact to notification. Firms in the information business may start limiting access to their information in an effort to reduce their risk exposure. Of particular concern is the prospect that the publicity associated with multiple notifications may induce consumers to shift their credit transactions offline, which the data show would actually increase their exposure to identity theft.

## The Effect on Competition

Many of the costs of privacy and data security regulations are likely to be relatively invariant with the size of the firm and therefore higher per unit of output for small than for large firms. Many of the costs are also what economists call "sunk" costs, which means they are not recoverable if, for example, the business fails. This is an added burden that will deter start-ups and could have an adverse effect on competition.

Most importantly, any regulation of the information sector that raises the costs of targeted advertising and obtaining accurate customer lists has a greater adverse effect on new entrants and small firms than it does on large, established firms. This is particularly true for Internet advertising, where established firms have lists of their own customers and visitors to their Web sites, but new firms must purchase such lists. As long as there is a market for customer lists and other such information, entrants can begin competing relatively easily. However, if regulation should reduce the size of the market and increase costs, competition from new entrants would be reduced.

## Federal vs. State Regulation

Given the nature of the Internet, regulation at the state level has the potential to produce additional costs and impede interstate commerce due to inconsistencies. A true federalist approach is not possible with markets and firms that are national, and even international, in scope. Firms will tend to comply with a single set of rules. In the absence of a preemptive federal statute, they will comply with the most stringent set of state regulations, which will in effect "preempt" other state regulations.

Without federal preemption, companies are still faced with the prospect of familiarizing themselves with numerous different state laws to make sure they are in compliance. The costs associated with this, which do not vary much with firm size, constitute a particular burden for smaller firms. Federal preemption of state privacy and data-security laws will reduce compliance costs and improve the benefit-cost balance.

The privacy debate represents some of the most complex policy-making challenges we have seen. This requires careful analysis of the actual proposals and their likely consequences to assure that, if adopted, their benefits are sufficient to justify their costs.

Thus far, and despite perceptions to the contrary, the evidence suggests that the market for personal information is working well and producing large benefits for consumers. Regulating in this rapidly changing technological environment, without evidence of significant market failure, runs the risk of adversely affecting innovation and slowing the progress of the IT [Information Technology] revolution, with potentially adverse implications for growth and productivity.

*"It's not just politicians who think cyber-terrorism is the future—it's terrorists as well."*

# Cyber-Terrorism Poses a Serious Threat to Global Security

**Simon Finch**

*In the following viewpoint, Simon Finch asserts that cyber-terrorism poses a serious threat to international security. He cites, for example, a cyber attack that threatened to shut down Estonia's government and financial institutions. Banks, power grids, broadcast satellites—many systems are vulnerable to attack, Finch maintains. Moreover, he claims, since almost all systems are interconnected, those networks not directly under attack are also vulnerable. Finch is co-author with Gabriel Range of the 2004 BBC2 drama,* The Man Who Broke Britain, *which examined fears of cyber-terrorism.*

As you read, consider the following questions:

1. Why, in Finch's view, were those in the cyber-security world believed to have a vested interest in exaggerating the Millennium Bug?

2. What are the only systems that are not physically connected to the Internet, according to the author?

3. Why does the author believe that control systems are a particular worry?

It now seems that John Reid [former Home Secretary, a position in British government similar to head of Homeland Security in the United States] wasn't scaremongering when he warned [in April 2007] of the growing cyber-terror threat facing Britain.

The three-week cyber-attack on Estonia threatened to black out the country's digital infrastructure as hackers broke through firewalls and infiltrated the Web sites of banks and political institutions. The result was chaos and one bank is still under sustained attack. Perhaps it's time to take the beleaguered Home Secretary seriously—on this matter, at least.

## Taking Cyber-Security Seriously

Dire predictions or widespread computer chaos are nothing new—remember the Millennium Bug?—but the threats were made and easily forgotten. Many in the cyber-security world—consultants seeking clients, academics chasing grants, companies selling software—were deemed to have a vested interest in exaggeration. As were politicians. Jack Straw [currently Lord High Chancellor and formerly Foreign Secretary] invoked the spectre or cyber-terror to help justify his 2001 anti-terrorism measures. By July that year, cyber-terrorism was in such vogue that President [George W.] Bush declared it a new threat for the near future. Barely seven weeks later, it was terrorists with box-cutters not keyboards that wreaked havoc, yet the White House's response was to bang the cyber drum still more.

Talk to those tasked with advising government on information security and, until now, most would have told you there was little concrete evidence that ideological hacking was heading for some big attack. A . . . report that the police had prevented an al-Qa'eda plot to attack Telehouse in Docklands, the biggest Internet hub in Europe, was apparently "overheated". But as computer security experts from NATO [North Atlantic Treaty Organization] the EU [European Union] and around the world land in Tallinn to learn what they can, it seems it's time to take cyber-security seriously.

## The Gravity of a Cyber Attack

The probability of an attack may yet be slim; but its potential gravity is huge. And it's not just politicians who think cyber-terrorism is the future—it's terrorists as well. In conversation with an American undercover agent working for MI5 [The United Kingdom's counter intelligence and security agency that is part of the government's intelligence services.], the leader of the Real IRA declared the future lay in "cyber-terrorism rather than car bombs".

Whether it is financial turmoil, power cuts, traffic chaos, hijacking into broadcast satellites or targeting logistics companies that deliver food to supermarkets, there are myriad possibilities for the determined "hacktivist" to contemplate.

Nuclear weapons and some of the most sensitive military systems may be "air-gapped", i.e. not physically connected to the Internet. But almost every other system is. All of the American (and British) battlefield systems are Internet-connected, since that's the easiest way to mesh them together. Hence the U.S. military, like the rest of us, is reliant on firewalls and encryption technologies to move sensitive information over a public network.

As one expert on ethical hacking puts it: "The problem nowadays is that, since the endemic spread of networks, almost all systems are interconnected; generally businesses now use firewalls as if they were air-gaps." What this means is that viruses can infect networks that are claimed to be entirely protected.

## The New Terrorism

The Internet, by its very nature, is an ideal arena for activity by terrorists; they tend to feel safer, because of perceived anonymity. It offers terrorists the advantage of greater security and operational flexibility. The mask of cyberspace provides terrorists the shield through which to cause widespread harm, as they can launch a computer assault from almost anywhere in the world without exposing the attacker to physical harm. More importantly, it's difficult to track a cyber-terrorist, as there is usually no physical evidence. It can be a low-budget form of attack, with the only real costs being computer equipment and programming time. This makes cyber-terrorism an attractive way to mount an attack. Unlike a real world attack, the terrorist needn't make or transport a bomb. Delivery may be as easy as a computer and Internet connection. In our computer dependent world, the potential targets are endless.

*Eberechi P. Ugwu,*
*"Cyberterrorism: The New Terrorism,"*
ISACA National Capital Area Chapter Newsletter,
*March 2007.*

According to the head of IT [Information Technology] security for one global investment house, a malicious virus recently simultaneously took out every single ATM of a major European bank. The network came down on a Friday, and it was only through some nifty footwork that it had the system up and running on Monday and prevented news of it leaking. As ever, the real worry was that the publicity surrounding the attack would have prompted withdrawals, which would have then created panic.

## Exploiting Ignorance

It is the Supervisory Control and Data Acquisition systems in power plants and similar industries that often give rise to "electronic Pearl Harbor" headlines. Control systems are a particular worry, because they are programs that manage physical processes, such as temperature and pressure regulation.

The good news is that wreaking real damage through them is likely to require insiders as well.

Part of the problem is how few people genuinely understand the consequences of our new, online world. A few technology companies are more than willing to exploit this ignorance, recasting themselves as providers of security expertise to the gullible and the rich.

Some of these outfits do very well for themselves, but the fees the genuine experts can command in this field are enormous. I asked one highly regarded encryption figure, who numbered Microsoft and the Pentagon among his clients, whether he did any work for our own Armed Forces. "Oh no, they can't afford me," he replied with a grin. Perhaps it's time to reconsider our defence budget.

> "Computer security specialists believe it is virtually impossible to use the Internet to inflict death on a large scale, and many scoff at the notion that terrorists would bother trying."

# The Problem of Cyberterrorism Is Exaggerated

*Joshua Green*

*Joshua Green argues that the threat of cyberterrorism has been exaggerated by the Bush administration ever since September 11, 2001. There has never been an instance of cyberterrorism, and yet cyberterrorism now ranks alongside other weapons of mass destruction in the public consciousness. The author asserts that governmental security is high, and that access to systems that remotely control an organization's processes or data acquisition is restricted. The real threat to national security, Green argues, is the tendency of the media to hype cyberterrorism. Eventually, the public will become immune to the warnings, and if one day, cyberterrorism really becomes a problem, the public will not heed the warnings. Joshua Green is an editor at* The Washington Monthly.

Joshua Green, "The Myth of Cyberterrorism," *Washington Monthly*, November 2002. Reproduced by permission.

As you read, consider the following questions:

1. According to Green, what are some of the less-protected second targets?

2. Why does the author assert that *The Washington Post's* June story on al Qaeda cyberterrorism was inaccurate?

3. According to the author, why is cyberterrorism hyped by the administration and the media?

Again and again since September 11 [2001], President Bush, Vice President Cheney, and senior administration officials have alerted the public not only to the dangers of chemical, biological, and nuclear weapons but also to the further menace of cyberterrorism. "Terrorists can sit at one computer connected to one network and can create worldwide havoc," warned Homeland Security Director Tom Ridge in a representative observation last April. "[They] don't necessarily need a bomb or explosives to cripple a sector of the economy, or shut down a power grid."

Even before September 11, Bush was fervently depicting an America imminently in danger of an attack by cyberterrorists, warning during his presidential campaign that "American forces are overused and underfunded precisely when they are confronted by a host of new threats and challenges—the spread of weapons of mass destruction, the rise of cyberterrorism, the proliferation of missile technology." In other words, the country is confronted not just by the specter of terrorism, but by a menacing new breed of it that is technologically advanced, little understood, and difficult to defend against. Since September 11, these concerns have only multiplied. A survey of 725 cities conducted by the National League of Cities for the anniversary of the attacks shows that cyberterrorism ranks with biological and chemical weapons atop officials' lists of fears.

Concern over cyberterrorism is particularly acute in Washington. As is often the case with a new threat, an entire industry has arisen to grapple with its ramifications—think tanks have launched new projects and issued white papers, experts have testified to its dangers before Congress, private companies have hastily deployed security consultants and software designed to protect public and private targets, and the media have trumpeted the threat with such front-page headlines as this one, in *The Washington Post* last June: "Cyber-Attacks by Al Qaeda Feared, Terrorists at Threshold of Using Internet as Tool of Bloodshed, Experts Say."

The federal government has requested $4.5 billion for infrastructure security next year [2002]; the FBI boasts more than 1,000 "cyber investigators"; President Bush and Vice President Cheney keep the issue before the public; and in response to September 11, Bush created the office of "cybersecurity czar" in the White House, naming to this position Richard Clarke, who has done more than anyone to raise awareness, including warning that "if an attack comes today with information warfare . . . it would be much, much worse than Pearl Harbor."

## Building a Culture of Fear

It's no surprise, then, that cyberterrorism now ranks alongside other weapons of mass destruction in the public consciousness. Americans have had a latent fear of catastrophic computer attack ever since a teenage Matthew Broderick hacked into the Pentagon's nuclear weapons system and nearly launched World War III in the 1983 movie *WarGames*. Judging by official alarums and newspaper headlines, such scenarios are all the more likely in today's wired world.

There's just one problem: There is no such thing as cyberterrorism—no instance of anyone ever having been killed by a terrorist (or anyone else) using a computer. Nor is there compelling evidence that al Qaeda or any other terrorist organization has resorted to computers for any sort of serious destructive activity. What's more, outside of a Tom Clancy novel, computer security specialists believe it is virtually impossible to use the Internet to inflict death on a large scale, and many scoff at the notion that terrorists would bother trying. "I don't lie awake at night worrying about cyber attacks ruining my life," says Dorothy Denning, a computer science professor at Georgetown University and one of the country's foremost cyber-security experts. "Not only does [cyberterrorism] not rank alongside chemical, biological, or nuclear weapons, but it is not anywhere near as serious as other potential physical threats like car bombs or suicide bombers."

Which is not to say that cyber security isn't a serious problem—it's just not one that involves terrorists. Interviews with terrorism and computer security experts, and current and former government and military officials, yielded near unanimous agreement that the real danger is from the criminals and other hackers who did $15 billion in damage to the global economy last year using viruses, worms, and other readily available tools. That figure is sure to balloon if more isn't done to protect vulnerable computer systems, the vast majority of which are in the private sector. Yet when it comes to imposing the tough measures on business necessary to protect against the real cyber threats, the Bush administration has balked.

## Cybersecurity

When ordinary people imagine cyberterrorism, they tend to think along Hollywood plot lines, doomsday scenarios in which terrorists hijack nuclear weapons, airliners, or military computers from halfway around the world. Given the colorful history of federal boondoggles—billion-dollar weapons systems that misfire, $600 toilet seats—that's an understandable concern. But, with few exceptions, it's not one that applies to preparedness for a cyber attack. "The government is miles ahead of the private sector when it comes to cybersecurity," says Michael Cheek, director of intelligence for iDefense, a

Virginia-based computer security company with government and private-sector clients. "Particularly the most sensitive military systems."

Serious effort and plain good fortune have combined to bring this about. Take nuclear weapons. The biggest fallacy about their vulnerability, promoted in action thrillers like *WarGames*, is that they're designed for remote operation. "[The movie] is premised on the assumption that there's a modem bank hanging on the side of the computer that controls the missiles," says Martin Libicki, a defense analyst at the RAND Corporation. "I assure you, there isn't." Rather, nuclear weapons and other sensitive military systems enjoy the most basic form of Internet security: they're "air-gapped," meaning that they're not physically connected to the Internet and are therefore inaccessible to outside hackers. (Nuclear weapons also contain "permissive action links," mechanisms to prevent weapons from being armed without inputting codes carried by the president.) A retired military official was somewhat indignant at the mere suggestion: "As a general principle, we've been looking at this thing for twenty years. What cave have you been living in if you haven't considered this [threat]?"

When it comes to cyber threats, the Defense Department has been particularly vigilant to protect key systems by isolating them from the Net and even from the Pentagon's internal network. All new software must be submitted to the National Security Agency for security testing. "Terrorists could not gain control of our spacecraft, nuclear weapons, or any other type of high-consequence asset," says Air Force Chief Information Officer John Gilligan. For more than a year, Pentagon CIO John Stenbit has enforced a moratorium on new wireless networks, which are often easy to hack into, as well as common wireless devices such as PDAs, BlackBerrys, and even wireless or infrared copiers and faxes.

The September 11 hijackings led to an outcry that airliners are particularly susceptible to cyberterrorism. Earlier this year,

## Cyber War Games

In October 2000, the Naval Postgraduate School hosted a conference to determine if terrorist groups would engage in cyberterrorism [School expert Dorothy] Denning said. Participants included academics, United Nations representatives, and most interestingly, a hacker and five representatives of "violent sub-state groups." The groups included the Palestine Liberation Organization, the Liberation Tigers of Tamil Eelan, the Basque Fatherland and Liberty Political/ Military Army, and the Revolutionary Armed Forces of Columbia. The group authorized an actual cyber attack during the game against the Russian stock exchange, Denning explained.

*Breanne Wagner, "Electronic Jihad: Experts Downplay Imminent Threat of Cyberterrorism,"* National Defense, *July 2007.*

for instance, Sen. Charles Schumer (D-N.Y.) described "the absolute havoc and devastation that would result if cyberterrorists suddenly shut down our air traffic control system, with thousands of planes in mid-flight." In fact, cybersecurity experts give some of their highest marks to the FAA, which reasonably separates its administrative and air traffic control systems and strictly air-gaps the latter. And there's a reason the 9/11 hijackers used box-cutters instead of keyboards: It's impossible to hijack a plane remotely, which eliminates the possibility of a high-tech 9/11 scenario in which planes are used as weapons.

Another source of concern is terrorist infiltration of our intelligence agencies. But here, too, the risk is slim. The CIA's classified computers are also air-gapped, as is the FBI's entire computer system. "They've been paranoid about this forever," says Libicki, adding that paranoia is a sound governing principle when it comes to cybersecurity. Such concerns are manifesting themselves in broader policy terms as well. One notable characteristic of last year's Quadrennial Defense Review was how strongly it focused on protecting information systems.

## Sensationalizing Weaknesses

That leaves the less-protected secondary targets—power grids, oil pipelines, dams, and water systems that don't present opportunities as nightmarish as do nuclear weapons, but nonetheless seem capable, under the wrong hands, of causing their own mass destruction. Because most of these systems are in the private sector and are not yet regarded as national security loopholes, they tend to be less secure than government and military systems. In addition, companies increasingly use the Internet to manage such processes as oil-pipeline flow and water levels in dams by means of "supervisory control and data acquisition" systems, or SCADA, which confers remote access. Most experts see possible vulnerability here, and though terrorists have never attempted to exploit it, media accounts often sensationalize the likelihood that they will.

To illustrate the supposed ease with which our enemies could subvert a dam, *The Washington Post's* June story on al Qaeda cyberterrorism related an anecdote about a twelve-year-old who hacked into the SCADA system at Arizona's Theodore Roosevelt Dam in 1998, and was, the article intimated, within mere keystrokes of unleashing millions of gallons of water upon helpless downstream communities. But a subsequent investigation by the tech-news site *CNet.com* revealed the tale to be largely apocryphal—the incident occurred in 1994, the hacker was twenty-seven, and, most importantly, investigators concluded that he couldn't have gained control of the dam and that no lives or property were ever at risk.

using the Internet to communicate and coordinate physical attacks. "There doesn't seem to be any evidence that the people we know as terrorists like to do cyberterrorism," says Libicki. Indeed, in a July report to the Senate Governmental Affairs Committee detailing the threats detected to critical infrastructure, the General Accounting Office noted "to date none of the traditional terrorist groups such as al Qaeda have used the Internet to launch a known assault on the U.S.'s infrastructure." It is much easier, and almost certainly much deadlier, to strike the old-fashioned way.

Yet Washington hypes cyberterrorism incessantly. "Cyberterrorism and cyberattacks are sexy right now. It's novel, original, it captures people's imagination," says Georgetown's Denning. Indeed, a peculiar sort of one-upmanship has developed when describing the severity of the threat. The most popular term, "electronic Pearl Harbor," was coined in 1991 by an alarmist tech writer named Winn Schwartau to hype a novel. For a while, in the mid-1990s, "electronic Chernobyl" was in vogue. Earlier this year, Sen. Charles Schumer (D-N.Y.) warned of a looming "digital Armageddon." And the Center for Strategic and International Studies, a Washington think tank, has christened its own term, "digital Waterloo."

Why all this brooding over so relatively minor a threat? Ignorance is one reason. Cyberterrorism merges two spheres—terrorism and technology—that most lawmakers and senior administration officials don't fully understand, and therefore, tend to fear, making them likelier to accede to any measure, if only out of self-preservation. Just as tellingly, many are eager to exploit this ignorance. Numerous technology companies, still reeling from the collapse of the tech bubble, have recast themselves as innovators crucial to national security and boosted their Washington presence in an effort to attract federal dollars. As Ohio State University law professor Peter Swire explained to *Mother Jones*, "Many companies that rode the dot-com boom need to find big new sources of income. One is direct sales to the federal government; another is federal mandates. If we have a big federal push for new security spending, that could prop up the sagging market."

But lately, a third motive has emerged: Stoking fears of cyberterrorism helps maintain the level of public anxiety about terrorism generally, which in turn makes it easier for the administration to pass its agenda.

> *"[Internet] piracy fundamentally threatens America's world-leading music, movie and software industries and the future of legitimate Internet commerce."*

# Internet Piracy Threatens the Entertainment Industry

*Orrin Hatch*

*In the following viewpoint, Orrin Hatch argues that Internet pirates illegally distribute billions of copies of valuable creative works. This piracy, he claims, poses a serious threat to the entertainment industry. Moreover, Hatch asserts, by encouraging others to download illegal copies, Internet pirates expose users to the risk of prosecution. In fact, he maintains, many of those who download copyrighted works do not realize that they are illegally distributing these files to strangers. Laws are necessary to punish those who profit from inducing others to infringe copyrights, Hatch reasons. Hatch is a U.S. Senator and chairman of the Senate Judiciary Committee.*

As you read, consider the following questions:

1. According to Hatch, what warnings does file-sharing software fail to provide users?

Orrin Hatch, "Efforts to Curb Illegal Downloading Copyrighted Music," Opening Statement of Chairman Orrin Hatch, Committee on Senate Judiciary, July 22, 2004. Reproduced by permission.

2. In the author's opinion, how does file-sharing software automate infringing redistribution of copyrighted works?

3. How, in the author's view, do pirates play one branch of the federal government against another?

For-profit global piracy rings ... threaten the future of today's cinema and recording industries. Research now suggests that these piracy rings—which call themselves file-sharing networks—will create between 12 and 24 billion infringing copies this year alone. This unprecedented level of piracy fundamentally threatens America's world-leading music, movie and software industries and the future of legitimate Internet commerce.

## The Architects of Piracy

The architects of this file-sharing piracy make millions of dollars while attempting to avoid any personal risk of the severe civil and criminal penalties for copyright infringement. I think all here today would agree that these pernicious schemes to encourage others—and unfortunately these are mostly kids—to break federal law allows these pirates to collect huge revenues while subjecting users to the risk of prison or crippling damage awards.

To implement their schemes, the architects of file-sharing piracy must encourage users to infringe copyrights in two different ways. First, they must encourage users to infringe copyrights by downloading infringing copies of works. This is an easy task because downloading users get for free valuable works that they would otherwise have to purchase. Unsurprisingly, the user interfaces of most file-sharing software provide no warnings about the prevalence of infringing files or the severity of the civil and criminal penalties for succumbing to the pervasive temptation to download them.

But infringing downloads cannot occur unless infringing files are available for download. The architects of file-sharing piracy must thus encourage users to infringe copyrights again by uploading files for distribution to millions of strangers. This is a difficult task: A user infringing by uploading gets nothing in return for his or her illegal act except a risk of prosecution.

## The Problem of Automatic Uploading

Free-riding downloaders are unlikely to become altruistic uploaders, so most file-sharing software automates the decision to upload: When used as intended, this software automatically redistributes every file downloaded. This makes uploading and redistribution automatic and invisible to the average user. This design ensures that while an infringing download requires a conscious choice, the separate and more dangerous infringing act of uploading usually does not.

Automatic uploading ensures that many free-riding downloaders will unwittingly turn their home computers into global piracy distribution centers. Harvard's Berkman Center for the Internet and Society warns that it can be extremely difficult for a non-expert computer user to shut down this automatic redistribution. The Center further warns that the complexity of Kazaa's installation and disabling functions can leave users unaware that they are distributing infringing files to potentially millions of strangers.

File-sharing software also automates infringing redistribution in other ways. For example, some distributors, like Bearshare, use installation wizards that—by default—cause users to redistribute every media file on their computer. This automatically turns people who have copied music CDs onto their computers for personal use into global redistributors of entire music collections. Such wizards can automatically create high-volume infringers and enforcement targets.

There can be no doubt that automating redistribution induces mass infringement that would otherwise never occur.

For example, here is the sworn testimony of one user of file-sharing software who lost her life savings in an uploading-related settlement:

> I never willingly shared files with other users.... As far as I was concerned, the music I downloaded was for home, personal use.... I downloaded songs I already owned on CD because I didn't want to mix them manually.... I don't know how to "upload" songs on the computer either. As far as I was concerned copyright infringement was what the people in Chinatown hawking bootlegged and fake CDs on the street corner were doing.

This testimony captures the problem: Unwitting consumers can break the law, subjecting themselves to significant liability and lawsuits that no one wants to be forced to bring.

## Delay and Obfuscation

The design of some file-sharing software thus enables its distributors to automate, induce, and profit from copyright piracy. We must stop these for-profit commercial piracy operations. They threaten the future of artists, legal commerce, and all but their most cautious and expert users. Indeed, I suspect that this piracy continues today only because its proponents have become adept at playing one branch of the federal government against another.

For example, Sharman Networks, the distributors of Kazaa, recently told the Ninth Circuit that courts must await legislative action on file-sharing piracy: Here, legislative action, not judicial law making, is particularly needed because political issues of comity are implicated in the legal subject matter. Yesterday, Sharman told Congress that legislative action on file-sharing piracy must await the courts: [I]t has been Congress' long-established practice to prudently refrain from intervening in active litigation. Passage of S. 2560, without awaiting final adjudication of [Grokster], would set the precedent for powerful interests to seek Congressional action challenging the outcomes of civil trials.

In short, Sharman is telling the courts that they must do nothing until Congress acts and then telling Congress that it must not act until the courts finish doing nothing. This tactic of delay and obfuscation is not isolated: In the appeal of Grokster, over forty-two parties and amici argued that judges must perpetuate any absurd results flowing from judge-made secondary-liability rules because only Congress has the competence to adjust these judge-made rules.

This exercise in self-contradiction may produce paralysis, but at a high price. Congress has always given courts flexibility to adapt secondary liability rules. Courts exercised that power most famously in the Sony-Betamax case. In Sony, a five-to-four majority of the Supreme Court altered the balance between copyrights and copying technologies by narrowing the prevailing secondary-liability rule. Sony narrowed that rule as to a small class of defendants by importing the substantial-noninfringing-use rule that Congress had codified only in the Patent Act. Consequently, anyone who argues that judges lack the competence to adjust secondary liability rules to balance the interests of copyrights and technology argues that Sony-Betamax is illegitimate and wrongly decided. I do not agree with that argument—and I doubt that its apparent proponents do either.

To address this problem, Senator [Patrick] Leahy and I introduced S. 2560, the Inducing Infringement of Copyrights Act.[1] The Act provides that the courts can impose secondary liability upon those who intend to induce copyright infringement. We developed this approach with the help and support of leading technology companies. We want to continue to work with interested parties to make refinements that will help us achieve the bill's intent.

1. The Inducing Infringement of Copyrights Act never left the Judiciary committee.

> "Internet piracy is more myth than reality—no more threatening to the music and film industries than the mechanical pirates at Disney World."

# The Problem of Internet Piracy Is Overstated

*Dave McClure*

*In the following viewpoint, Dave McClure claims that there is more myth than reality to the threat of Internet piracy. Because determining actual losses is difficult, Hollywood overstates the problem to promote unnecessary copyright legislation, he maintains. McClure claims that Hollywood makes these exaggerated claims because it cannot cope with the impact of the Internet and fears losing its power over artists and their creative works claims. He asserts that the Internet, however, is not likely to bend to the will of Hollywood. McClure is a software developer, entrepreneur, and consultant who writes about technology issues.*

As you read, consider the following questions:

1. In McClure's view, who is actually responsible for a vast majority of Internet piracy?

Dave McClure, "Internet Piracy," The *CPA Technology Advisor*, vol. 14, December 2004, p. 52. Copyright © 2004 Cygnus Business Media. All rights reserved. Reproduced by permission.

2. What are some of the results that have followed from revision of America's copyright laws, in the author's opinion?

3. What does the author say Hollywood had done while struggling to sort out how to deal with the Internet?

A vast, ye lubbers, there be pirates on the Internet! Blood-thirsty pirates, cruel and rapacious pirate, pirates who steal the very bread from the mouths of innocent artists.

That's how Hollywood tells it, anyway. But there's a growing realization that Internet piracy is more myth than reality—no more threatening to the music and film industries than the mechanical pirates at Disney World.

The way Hollywood tells it, Internet pirates steal the best creative works before the artists can even make a living. They warn that unless this piracy is thwarted, it simply won't be worth their time to make any more music or films. In fact, producer/director George Lucas told Congress that without more laws to stop Internet piracy, the world would never see another Star Wars epic. (Having seen the last two he produced, I'm kind of hoping he keeps that promise. But that's another issue.)

## Questioning the Claims

The technology media, starved for news in a year with virtually no new products to talk about, dutifully report that the end of the world is nigh because of Internet piracy. But were they to do the least bit of research, they'd discover that the issue of Internet piracy is a lot less than meets the eye. In fact, there is good cause to question whether it exists at all.

Sure, there is some piracy of copyrighted works. But if you peel away all of the nonsense and hysteria, it turns out that the vast majority of the piracy is by studio insiders, not Internet pirates. It's organized gangs of video criminals who are hurting the studios, not teens using Kazaa. If the studios are

## Artists Say the Internet Has Been a Boon

- 23% of all online artists and 45% of paid online artists [those who are compensated for their art] report using the Internet or e-mail to promote, advertise or display their art.

- 23% of all online artists and 41% of paid online artists say they personally use the Internet or e-mail to keep in touch with fans of their art.

- 21% of all online artists and 44% of paid online artists use the Internet to schedule performances and other promotional events.

- 20% of all online artists and 38% of paid online artists say they have used the Internet or e-mail to provide free samples or previews of their art to the public.

*Mary Madden, Artists, Musicians and the Internet*
*[Pew Internet & American Life Project], December 5, 2004.*

being hurt at all. With the economy recovering, sales of music and videos are escalating nicely, destroying Hollywood's claim that Internet piracy was somehow hurting sales. What's more, the piracy losses described by film and music industry lobbyists—billions of dollars in losses each year—are a pure and simple lie.

There may be losses, and there may not be. There is no way to validate the losses or even determine whether there are any, so Hollywood just makes up big, scary numbers each year and tries to avoid questions about how the numbers were derived. I know, because I used to be part of one of the organizations that made up the numbers. I've seen it with my own eyes.

## Unnecessary Penalties

All of this might be just another bad Hollywood script if there weren't politicians who take it seriously. Each year, for the past decade, the Congress has dutifully created ever-harsher penalties and expanded the definitions of copyright infringement in an effort to find some Internet pirates and punish them. Word is that they will be back at it again . . . in an effort to re-write America's copyright laws once again.

You don't have to look very far to see how lunatic this situation has become. Carry a cell phone with video recording capabilities with you to a movie theater and you are in violation of federal law. The Girl Scouts were sued over songs the girls sang around the campfire for infringement on music copyrights. More than 5,000 consumers, including some who don't have a computer, have been sued by the music industry for pirating music over the Internet.

## The Disruptive Power of the Internet

But if Internet piracy is mostly a myth, why does Hollywood continue to make it a favored whipping boy? And why take the enormous risk of committing perjury in an effort to convince the world that it is real?

The Internet is one of the most disruptive technologies since the printing press. And, just as the Gutenberg Press destroyed forever the power of the Catholic Church, the Internet will change forever our view of copyrights and ownership of content. It will destroy the power of the music and film industries over their artists and artistic works.

Hollywood is reeling from the impact of the Internet, with no idea how to keep pace with the change or profit from the technology. While they struggle to sort it out, they have launched their legions of lawyers in an effort to stop the introduction of new technologies and tighten their control over how music, video and books are made available to consumers.

Ultimately, these efforts will fall as saner heads prevail. But the goal of Hollywood is not to win; it is to stall until they have time to figure it out. Sadly, legal strategies are unlikely to buy them the time they want. The Internet is what it is and will be, and doesn't easily bend to shape the wishes of Hollywood executives.

"*Sexual predation over the Internet is a serious problem according to law enforcement agencies and online experts.*"

# Online Predators Are a Serious Threat

## Jeff Buckstein

*In the following viewpoint, Canadian journalist Jeff Buckstein maintains that law enforcement and Internet experts agree that online predators pose a serious threat to children. In fact, he claims, the problem may be even more widespread, as only 10 percent of those who receive sexual solicitations on the Internet actually report the crime. According to Buckstein, online predators easily recognize signs of vulnerability in their young victims, including loneliness and difficulties at home. He concludes that online experts recommend parents take an active role in their children's computer use to reduce the chance that their children will become victims.*

As you read, consider the following questions:

1. In Buckstein's opinion, why was Alicia Kozakiewicz lucky?

2. What did a survey of Canadian students in grades four through eleven reveal, according to the author?

3. What do some experts say parents need to consider installing, in the author's view?

Alicia Kozakiewicz was, by her own admission, a normal "very shy" teenaged girl who enjoyed chatting online, and felt slightly emboldened by the anonymity of the Internet, which "allows a timid child to miraculously transform themselves."

But on Jan. 1, 2002, Kozakiewicz, who was thirteen at the time, experienced firsthand the horrors of what can go wrong on the Internet. She was lured from her Pittsburgh home, then abducted and driven to the Virginia townhouse of Scott Tyree, thirty-eight, a computer programmer.

Tyree, who is serving a nineteen-year, seven-month prison sentence for abduction, torture and rape, targeted Kozakiewicz, with whom he'd corresponded online after being introduced by a friend. The friend had gotten through to her posing as a fourteen-year-old girl named "Christine."

"We became the very best of friends. We shared all of our thoughts and intimate girlhood secrets. There was nothing 'she' didn't know about me," Kozakiewicz, now nineteen and a university sophomore studying forensic psychology, told the U.S. House of Representatives Judiciary Committee in October 2007. But "Christine was really a middle-aged pervert."

Kozakiewicz was lucky. She was rescued four days later after Tyree sent online photos of his captive to an Internet acquaintance, who immediately called the Federal Bureau of Investigation [FBI]. Working feverishly to match the service provider and geographic location, the FBI quickly located Kozakiewicz and arrested Tyree at work.

Had they not done so, she believes Tyree was ready to kill her.

## A Lesson for Others

Nicole had barely turned twelve when a twenty-nine-year-old man crept into her bedroom.

His entry point was her PC. His ticket was AOL Instant Messenger. His method was to befriend her through online chats, lure her from home and molest her.

It took a month for him to accomplish it all. . . .

Though the predator was arrested, and police say he confessed, he is a fugitive.

Now, Nicole and her mother seek their own kind of justice. They want to make sure the mistakes made by prosecutors at the time—allowing Waqas "Michael" Rehman to flee the country before being brought to justice—won't happen again. And they want Nicole's story to be a lesson for others.

*Daniel Vasquez,* South Florida Sun-Sentinel, *April 20, 2008.*

While that's an extreme case, sexual predation over the Internet is a serious problem according to law enforcement agencies and online experts.

The National Centre for Missing and Exploited Children (NCMEC) in Alexandria, [Virginia], received more than 191 leads concerning child exploitation online during a one-week period in mid-February—second only behind the possession, manufacturing and distribution of child pornography, says John Shehan, the NCMEC's deputy director of Exploited Children's Services.

The numbers may actually be much higher because studies show that as few as 10 percent of individuals who receive online solicitations actually report them, adds Shehan.

The NCMEC study Online Victimization of Youth, released in 2006, says about one in seven children receive unwanted online sexual solicitations, with a majority of those aimed at females in the fourteen to seventeen year age group. The organization has therefore launched advertising campaigns aimed at youth with the themes Don't Believe the Type and Think Before You Post. The latter is in response to a "spike in pornographic images being self-produced by teenagers," says Shehan, who explains that once posted online, those images "are out there forever."

A survey of Canadian students in grades four through eleven by the Ottawa-based Media Awareness Network in 2005 revealed that 22 percent of Canadian children surveyed had a personal Web cam, and that number jumped to 31 percent by grade eleven. "That's where we always stop and ask, 'Why would parents let their kids have a Web cam?'" asks RCMP superintendent Earla-Kim McColl, who heads up the RCMP's National Child Exploitation Coordination Centre.

But even something as seemingly innocuous as simple conversation can grab a predator's attention, as Kozakiewicz' case illustrates.

Experts stress that predators easily pick up signs of vulnerability, such as loneliness, lack of close interpersonal relationships, or difficulties at home, and warn children and adolescents against posting revealing information online, lest they attract the wrong person.

Cyber-bullying is another serious problem that can cause serious psychological damage and, in extreme cases, has led to suicide.

In October 2006, Megan Meier, a Missouri girl two weeks shy of her fourteenth birthday, hanged herself after seemingly being berated by a young man she had befriended and formed an emotional attachment with online. The young man, who gave his name as 'Josh Evans' turned out to be a hoax perpetrated by a female classmate, along with the classmate's mother and an older girl.

While the Meier case was, in many ways, "very unusual and quite extraordinary," it did feature some of the real dangers associated with cyber-bullying, says Stephen Balkam, chief executive officer of the Family Online Safety Institute in Washington, D.C.

For instance, cyber-bullying usually initially involves people who know one another, typically through school, and spreads so that others, some of whom may not be acquaintances, join in and gang up on the victim. That can be "very traumatic for a child" on the receiving end, Balkam adds.

To limit the chance their child may become victimized by cyber-bullying or sexual predators, experts recommend parents insist the home computer be located in a common area, such as the family room or kitchen, where they can better monitor what's going on.

But while that might reduce threats, it can't eliminate them. In an interview, Mary Kozakiewicz, Alicia's mother, said the computer in their home was located in a common room at the time of her daughter's abduction. What they weren't aware of, however, was that Alicia "was online at night"— something she and her husband would have forbidden had they known at the time.

For Internet usage within the home, experts say parents also need to consider installing monitoring software that will provide a list of Web sites, and in some cases, screen captures of what their adolescents are viewing online. They acknowledge, however, that the competing needs for privacy and protection can be very delicate, involving issues of ethics and trust.

If a parent finds that their child has been victimized—and potential warning signs include very long times sitting alone at the computer, excessive moodiness and unwillingness to communicate—they need to first talk to their child to try and find out what the problem is.

> "The stereotype of the Internet child mo-
> lester who uses trickery and violence to
> assault children is largely inaccurate."

# The Media Stereotype of Online Predators Is Inaccurate

*Janis Wolak, David Finkelhor, Kimberly J. Mitchell,
and Michele L. Ybarra*

*In the following viewpoint, researchers Janis Wolak, David
Finkelhor, Kimberly J. Mitchell, and Michele L. Ybarra claim
that few online sex crimes are perpetrated by pedophiles who are
deceptive and violent. In fact, the authors assert, most Internet
sex crimes are initiated by men interested in consensual sex with
teens too young to consent. These criminals rarely pretend to be
teens and are even more rarely violent, the authors maintain.
Having a more accurate picture of Internet sex crimes will improve how mental health professionals and law enforcement respond to these crimes, the authors reason. Wolak, Finkelhor, and
Mitchell represent the Crimes Against Children Research Center
at the University of New Hampshire. Ybarra works for Internet
Solutions for Kids, Inc.*

As you read, consider the following questions:

1. In the authors' opinion, what do most victims who meet offenders face-to-face expect to do?

2. Why would it be difficult for pedophiles to use the Internet to target young children directly, in the authors' opinion?

3. According to the authors, how are those who solicited undercover investigators different from other online offenders?

The research about Internet-initiated sex crimes makes it clear that the stereotype of the Internet child molester who uses trickery and violence to assault children is largely inaccurate. Most Internet-initiated sex crimes involve adult men who use the Internet to meet and seduce underage adolescents into sexual encounters. The offenders use Internet communications such as instant messages, e-mail, and chat rooms to meet and develop intimate relationships with victims. In the great majority of cases, victims are aware they are conversing online with adults. In the N-JOV [National Juvenile Online Victimization] Study, only 5 percent of offenders pretended to be teens when they met potential victims online. Also, offenders rarely deceive victims about their sexual interests. Sex is usually broached online, and most victims who meet offenders face to face go to such meetings expecting to engage in sexual activity. Many victims profess love or close feelings for offenders. In the N-JOV Study, 73 percent of victims who had face-to-face sexual encounters with offenders did so more than once. When deception does occur, it often involves promises of love and romance by offenders whose intentions are primarily sexual. Most offenders are charged with crimes, such as statutory rape, that involve nonforcible sexual activity with victims who are too young to consent to sexual intercourse with adults. . . .

The widespread popularity of television shows such as *To Catch a Predator* reveals the public fascination with online child molesters. The media has been quick to characterize such men as Internet or online "predators" and pedophiles. Implicit in these characterizations is the notion that these are highly motivated and repetitive sex offenders who have deviant sexual interests in children and predilections to abduction and violent assault. In fact, the considerable research and theory about child molesters—on what impels them to offend, how likely they are to have large numbers of victims or to re-offend, and whether they have violent propensities—makes it clear that child molesters are, in reality, a diverse group that cannot be accurately characterized with one-dimensional labels. Although there is little research specifically about *online* child molesters, there are indications that they occupy a narrow range on the spectrum of the sex offender population, one that largely excludes pedophiles and violent or sadistic offenders.

## Online Child Molesters Are Generally Not Pedophiles

Because online child molesters primarily target adolescents, not young children, such offenders do not fit the clinical profile of pedophiles, who are, by definition, sexually attracted to prepubescent children. For several reasons, it would be difficult for pedophiles to use the Internet to target and recruit young children directly. Young children are not as accessible online as adolescents. They use the Internet less for communication, and they are more supervised in their online activities. Also, they are less likely to respond to overtures from online child molesters because they are, for developmental reasons, less interested in relationships, sex, and romance than are adolescents. Although cases of pedophiles using the Internet to meet prepubescent victims directly are quite rare, such offenders do use the Internet in other ways. For example, some pedophiles get access to young child victims through online contact with parents or other adult offenders, or they use the Internet to acquire child pornography. . . .

## Online Child Molesters Are Rarely Violent

Violence is rare in Internet-initiated sex crimes. The evidence from the N-JOV Study suggests that online molesters are not among that minority of child offenders who abduct or assault victims because they have sadistic tendencies or lack the interpersonal skills to gain the confidence and acquiescence of victims. Most online child molesters are patient enough to develop relationships with victims and savvy enough to move those relationships offline. They know what to say to teens to gain their trust, arouse their sexual interest, and maintain relationships through face-to-face meetings. Abduction is also rare. None of the victims in the N-JOV Study was abducted in the sense of being forced to accompany offenders. However, about one quarter of the cases started with missing persons reports because victims ran away to be with offenders or lied to parents about their whereabouts. So, in many cases, abduction may have been feared.

This is not to say that online child molesters are never violent or never abduct. In the N-JOV Study, 5 percent used threats or violence, mostly forcible or attempted rape. In at least one highly publicized Internet-initiated case, a 13-year-old girl was murdered. Abductions have occurred as well but are very unusual. Overall, what we know about online child molesters suggests that they are not generally impulsive, aggressive, or violent. One possible explanation is that Internet use in the early 2000s was concentrated among those with technical skills, higher educations, and higher incomes, statuses hard to attain by those with impulsive and violent inclinations. This pattern may be changing as Internet access and skills become more widely disseminated. On the other hand, the Internet may never be conducive to antisocial offender styles involving impulse and intimidation, because initial interactions are remote, physical contact is not certain, and intimidation may be difficult to project. Nonetheless, video Web cameras and other technologies that introduce sight and sound into online communications are becoming more sophisticated. It remains to be seen whether they could make the Internet a more attractive venue for antisocial offenders.

## The Offenders in Undercover "Sting" Operations

In the year covered by the N-JOV Study, more online molesters were arrested for soliciting undercover investigators posing online as adolescents than were arrested for soliciting actual youths. These offenders also appeared to be different from other online molesters to some extent. Those who solicited undercover investigators were somewhat older and more middle class in income and employment compared with those who solicited actual youths. They were also somewhat less likely to have prior arrests for sexual offenses against minors or for nonsexual offenses or to have histories of violence or deviant sexual behavior. However, both groups had equally high rates of child pornography possession (about 40 percent) and rates of substance abuse (about 15 percent). Moreover, one in eight offenders arrested in undercover operations had also committed crimes against actual youth victims, which were discovered as a result of the undercover operation. It may be that the offenders most likely to be fooled by undercover investigators lack suspicion about law enforcement because they have less criminal experience and higher social status. It could also be that some such individuals are less experienced or skilled and more naive in their pursuit of youths and are thus more easily caught.

## Child Pornography and Exhibitionism

Child pornography (i.e., sexually explicit images of children younger than eighteen) may play a role in Internet-initiated sex crimes that is different from the role it has played in of-fline sexual offending. In the N-JOV Study, 39 percent of on-line child molesters possessed child pornography, a felony un-der federal law and in most states. Whereas child pornography is not a new phenomenon, the advent of the Internet has changed its nature as a crime problem. Child pornography possession, which used to be seen as a low-incidence crime committed almost exclusively by those with an enduring sexual interest in children, has evolved into a more general crime problem with an increasingly diverse array of offenders who can access and circulate images easily and privately from home computers. The small amount of research about the motiva-tions of child pornography possessors suggests that, among other purposes, it is used to fuel sexual fantasy, enhance mas-turbation, and groom and seduce victims, and sometimes it is accessed out of curiosity or for its shock value.

Child pornography *production* is also an aspect of Internet-initiated sex crimes. One in five online child molesters in the N-JOV Study took sexually suggestive or explicit photographs of victims or convinced victims to take such photographs of themselves or friends. In the YISS-2 [Youth Internet Safety Survey 2], 4 percent of youth Internet users were asked to take sexual pictures of themselves and send them to online solici-tors. Many of these requests appeared to constitute produc-tion of child pornography under federal statutes. In addition, if youths comply with such requests, solicitors and others can circulate the images widely online with no possibility that cir-culation can be curtailed. This is a situation some youths might not have the foresight to understand or appreciate.

The Internet also may be particularly attractive to offend-ers with exhibitionistic tendencies, who can use Web cameras to transmit images of themselves online. In the N-JOV Study, 18 percent of online child molesters sent photos of themselves in sexual poses to victims. In the YISS-2, 6 percent of youths who were sexually solicited received such pictures from solici-tors.

## Tragic Misdirection

The issue is not whether children need to be protected; of course they do. The issues are whether the danger to them is great, and whether the measures proposed will ensure their safety. While some efforts—such as longer sentences for repeat offenders—are well-reasoned and likely to be effective, those focused on separating sex offenders from the public are of little value because they are based on a faulty premise. Simply knowing where a released sex offender lives—or is at any given moment—does not ensure that he or she won't be near potential victims. Since relatively few sexual assaults are committed by released sex offenders, the concern over the danger is wildly disproportionate to the real threat. Efforts to protect children are well-intentioned, but legislation should be based on facts and reasoned argument instead of fear in the midst of a national moral panic.

*Benjamin Radford,*
*"Predator Panic: A Closer Look,"*
Skeptical Inquirer, *September 2006.*

Several technological developments could facilitate continuing increases in child pornography possession, distribution, and production, as well as the use of the Internet by exhibitionists. In the future, all three of these problems may be exacerbated by the growing capacity of computers and removable media to store images; wireless technologies that create mobile access to the Internet via portable devices; widespread access to digital photography, including cell phones and other handheld devices that take and transmit photos; and the increasing use of video Web cameras in chat rooms and during one-on-one communications such as through instant messages.

Concern about the Internet has fostered speculation that it may increase the number of "hands on" sex offenders and the number of youths victimized, above and beyond the growth in offenses related to possession of child pornography. Although there are plausible mechanisms by which this could happen, they remain speculations as yet unsupported by research findings. . . .

## Sex Crimes Against Youths Have Not Increased

An important fact that supports caution in speculating about how the Internet has facilitated child molestation is that several sex crime and abuse indicators have shown marked declines during the same period that Internet use has been expanding. From 1990 to 2005, the number of sex abuse cases substantiated by child protective authorities declined 51 percent, along with other related indicators. For example, the rate of sexual assaults reported by teenagers to the National Crime Victimization Survey declined by 52 percent between 1993 and 2005. A statewide survey of students in Minnesota also showed declines in sexual abuse during this period. Other indicators that might reflect on sexual victimization have also improved. The rate of pregnancy among teenagers has declined; there have been fewer delinquency arrests and fewer children running away from home. To claim, as one headline from Newsweek did, that the Internet has fostered a "shocking increase in the sexual exploitation of children," one has to explain why this epidemic has not been more apparent in aggregate indicators of juvenile sexual victimization.

One possibility is that sex offenders have migrated to the Internet from other environments, so that increases in online sex offending have been balanced by decreases in offline victimizations. It is also possible that Internet-initiated sex crimes have increased dramatically but are still relatively few in number compared with offline sex crimes. If so, a serious rise in sex crimes facilitated by the Internet may come in the future as the Internet continues to expand its influence. It may also be that the Internet is only affecting the subgroup of nonforcible sex crimes against adolescents, which are not well measured by most crime indicators because they typically focus on forcible offenses. Or it could be that the Internet factors that hypothetically facilitate sex crimes are not as prevalent or powerful as some believe or are counteracted by other factors that inhibit sex crimes.

Clearly, more research is needed on these issues. Because Internet-initiated sex crimes are a relatively new phenomenon, it may take some time before there is enough information to understand their role and relationship to juvenile sexual victimization overall. In the meantime, it is premature to talk about the Internet as an established facilitator of sex crimes, beyond the possession and distribution of child pornography.

# Periodical Bibliography

*The following articles have been selected to supplement the diverse views presented in this chapter.*

*Credit Union Journal*  "ID Theft Fear? Up. Awareness? Up. Actual Cases? Down," February 26, 2007.

Monique F. Einhorn  "Coping with Identity Theft," *Partners in Community and Economic Development*, Summer 2005.

Mark Gibbs  "Big Entertainment Is the New Threat," *Network World*, July 2, 2007.

Dan Ilett  "The Enemy at the Cyber-Gates," *Computer Weekly*, July 17, 2007.

Peter Katel  "Identity Theft," *CQ Researcher*, June 10, 2005.

Poonam Khanna  "Cybercrime on the Rise: A New Report Breaks Down the Range of Online Wrongdoers and the Most Popular Ways to Dupe Cybersurfers," *Computer Dealer News*, August 5, 2005.

Edie G. Lush  "How Cyber-Crime Became a Multi-Billion-Pound Industry," *Spectator*, June 16, 2007.

James A. Lyons  "Asymmetric Cyber Threat," *Washington Times*, November 13, 2007.

McAfee, Inc.  *Virtual Criminology Report*, 2007.

Michael Stohl  "Cyber Terrorism: A Clear and Present Danger, The Sum of All Fears, Breaking Point or Patriot Games?" *Crime, Law & Social Change*, 2006.

Eberechi P. Ugwu  "Cyberterrorism: The New Terrorism," *ISACA, National Capital Area Chapter Newsletter*, March 2007.

Breanne Wagner  "Experts Downplay Imminent Threat of Cyberterrorism," *National Defense*, July 2007.

**OPPOSING VIEWPOINTS® SERIES**

# CHAPTER 2

# What Factors Contribute to Cyber Crime?

# Chapter Preface

Computer hackers' motives vary. "Black-hat" hackers break into computer systems to steal or to create problems. "White-hat" hackers break into the computers of companies that employ them to help these companies improve the state of their technology. In between these two extremes is the "gray-hat" hacker. These hackers do not intend to inflict damage or steal. The goal of the "gray-hat" hackers is to point out vulnerabilities so that companies will take their computer security more seriously. Some "gray-hat" hackers may even publicize their hacking codes, called "scripts," on the Internet. Still other "gray-hat" hackers have made a business of hacking and revealing software vulnerabilities. Not everyone approves of "gray-hat" hackers' methods. According to Martha Stansell-Gamm, chief of the Department of Justice's Computer Crime and Intellectual Property division, "Thanking hackers who violate the privacy of networks or network users [by] pointing out our vulnerabilities is a little bit like sending thank-you notes to burglars for pointing out the infirmity of our physical alarms." Indeed, one of several controversies in the debate over what factors contribute to cyber crime is whether companies that expose security vulnerabilities improve network security or increase these problems.

Some experts argue that publicizing software vulnerabilities gives users a way to protect themselves against cyber criminals who exploit these flaws. Moreover, these commentators claim, disclosure compels software makers to distribute software "patches" that will fix these security problems. In addition, they maintain, exposing vulnerabilities motivates software vendors to create more secure products. "I'm very big on disclosure because it advances the security posture of everyone," argues computer security expert Victor Keong. "The earlier that [software merchants] get the patches out there, the better," he reasons. Most companies that expose software vulnerabilities agree. "BugNet is very solutions-oriented," general manager Eric Bowden asserts. "We're not in it to point fingers or play the blame-game with [software] developers as much as we're trying to find solutions to serious problems," he explains.

Some software security analysts such as Microsoft's Scott Culp dispute the protection offered by the disclosure of vulnerabilities. "It's simply indefensible for the security community to continue arming cyber criminals," Culp claims. "We can and should discuss security vulnerabilities," he agrees, "but we should be smart, prudent, and responsible in the way we do it." Microsoft has formed an alliance with several bug-hunting companies to restrict the publication of software flaws. Alliance members agree to wait at least thirty days before publicizing software vulnerabilities. According to Eddie Schwartz, of alliance member Guardent Inc., "We want to create an atmosphere where people are more responsible with the disclosure of vulnerability information." Not all security experts agree. "I think the thirty-day grace period is just another way for Microsoft and others to once again remove themselves from their responsibility for developing quality software before it hits the streets," claims John Cowan of Caldwell Industries, Inc.

Security experts such as Schwartz and Cowan continue to debate whether public disclosure improves the security of software or actually makes consumers and business more vulnerable. The authors in the following chapter examine other factors that they claim contribute to cyber crime.

> *"Attack technologies are readily available on the Web, meaning that virtually anyone, aided by a well-placed associate with access, can launch a successful insider attack on a company..."*

# Organizational Mismanagement, Not Hackers, Explain Most Data Breaches

*Frank Washkuch Jr.*

*While many believe that computer hackers are to blame for personal data security breaches, Frank Washkuch Jr. asserts in the following viewpoint, organizational mismanagement is more often to blame. Washkuch reveals that insider theft is much more common than infiltration by a hacker not involved in the company. Since attack technologies are now easily accessible on the Internet, virtually anyone can launch an attack. Washkuch argues that instead of placing time and energy into security features, Information Technology (IT) professionals should make sure they can trust who they are working with. Frank Washkuch has been a reporter for* SC Magazine *since 2005.*

As you read, consider the following questions:

1. According to the viewpoint, what are some possible portable devices that could serve as attack tools?
2. Why does Washkuch argue that a careless employee can be just as dangerous as a vengeful one?
3. What is the best way to combat insider risks, according to the author?

The new employee in human resources. The long-time company loyalist in the finance department. The temp working nearby. And now, more contract employees brought on to save on costs associated with hiring full-time staff.

For IT [Information Technology] pros charged with protecting a company from insider loss or theft of critical data, each of these employees is a potential risk—even the ones who are far from looking like the stereotypical disgruntled employee.

And besides intentional insider theft of sensitive data or simple error that leads to exposures, corporate security practitioners have still additional threats to which they must pay attention. With the help of readily available tools on the Internet and a trusted insider looking for a cut of the take, cyber criminals have plenty of methods at their disposal to steal crucial money-making data. Phishing e-mails, portable storage devices like iPods and USB drives, or other attack tools— along with some inside assistance—can make it that much easier for cyber thieves to get their hands on corporate info for either use or resale, according to many experts.

On top of these threats, companies that provide customers with convenient home-based services—and give third-party vendors access to sensitive information from multiple locations with little oversight—are unintentionally placing themselves at increased risk of an insider-prompted breach, according to Sam Curry, vice president of product management and product marketing at RSA, the security division of EMC.

## Insiders Pose the Real Threat

"Companies are looking to roll out more services and to get more out of their data, and the big obstacle to that is security. First, the data is more mobile, and second, the bad guys are more organized," he says.

The case of Gary Min, a former DuPont employee who was sentenced to eighteen months in prison after he pleaded guilty to stealing more than $400 million in trade secrets, is a much-cited example of a corporate insider gone wrong. Once a high-ranking scientist at the Delaware-based company, Min attempted to take his wrongfully accessed information to his new employer.

However, a careless employee can be just as dangerous as a vengeful one. A worker who brings a laptop home, disregarding company policy, or leaves it in their automobile, could be placing the personal information of millions of employees or customers at risk. While yesterday's criminals were after the laptops themselves, today's bad eggs realize the importance of the data stored on them, according to Ted Julian, VP of marketing at Application Security, Inc.

"The bad guys have gone pro, and they're after data that they can sell, and that's what's driven the north-of-250-million records compromised over the past two years, and it's also triggered a change in tactics in what they're targeting and their methods in targeting that data," he says. "The dilemma that enterprises face: it could be the well placed attacker, it could be the rogue insider with an iPod, and it could be that the insider has an accomplice, or it could be the employee who unwittingly gets phished."

## Trust, But Verify

Some business trends intended to help corporations save money and personnel power may have an unintentionally harmful effect on network and data security. The increased use of third-party vendors has changed the definition of who are considered insiders by security professionals, according to Ivan Arce, chief technology officer at Core Technologies.

"Another problem is [the question of] who's an insider, because there are so many initiatives that you outsource, you don't know who's an insider and who's not an insider anymore," he says. "In terms of protection, you can see that the industry is reacting in certain ways—NAC, policy enforcement—and, on the other hand, you can see a whole bunch of other things with productivity and identity management. You see different attempts at addressing the problem, but none of them that I know of are the silver-bullet solution. There is no technology solution by itself."

## Virtually Anyone Can Launch an Attack

Cyber criminals also have a number of new advantages when launching insider-based attacks. Attack technologies are readily available on the Web, meaning that virtually anyone, aided by a well-placed associate with access, can launch a successful insider attack on a company, says Steve Davis, consultant at Mandiant, an incident-response organization.

"They're becoming a lot easier. It's not even a penetration test. It's really just going on the Internet and running a tool and you're done," says Jones. "All you have to have is the Internet."

The relative ease of pulling off an insider-aided attack, along with the myriad reports of data loss on the front pages of newspapers and Web sites, indicates that most IT professionals are aware of the threat posed by a disgruntled employee. For them, a bigger challenge is convincing a corporate executive in charge of the company purse strings that employee monitoring is just as high a priority as other threats, says Julian.

"Everybody is aware. I don't think awareness is the issue. I think it's constrained budget and the difficulties of changing priorities. It's not an easy conversation to have to go to a CEO

**Security Breaches Hit Facilities Nationwide**

| Date | Name | Type of breach | Number of people affected |
|------|------|----------------|---------------------------|
| June 6, 2005 | CitiFinancial | Lost backup tapes | 3,900,000 |
| May 28, 2005 | Merlin Data Services | Bogus accounts set up | 9,000 |
| May 4, 2005 | Colorado Health Department | Stolen laptop | 1,600 (families) |
| May 2, 2005 | Time Warner | Lost backup tapes | 600,000 |
| April 28, 2005 | Georgia Southern University | Hacking | "ten of thousands" |
| April 28, 2005 | Wachovia, Bank of America, PNC Financial Services Group | Dishonest insiders | 676,000 |
| April 21, 2005 | Carnegie Mellon University | Hacking | 19,000 |
| April 20, 2005 | Ameritrade | Lost backup tape | 200,000 |
| April 18, 2005 | DSW/Retail Ventures | Hacking | 1,300,000 |
| April 14, 2005 | Polo Ralph Lauren/HSBC | Hacking | 180,000 |
| April 12, 2005 | LexisNexis | Passwords compromised | Additional 280,000 |

TAKEN FROM: Privacy Rights Clearinghouse.

and say that the $3 million we spent last year isn't relevant because the threats have changed," he says. "Another trend I highlight is that [IT pros are] tying this to compliance budgets, because those are budgets you can quite easily drive for."

With challenges such as tight budgets, the use of third parties, already constrained internal resources, and more proficient cyber criminals, IT professionals require a multifaceted response to insider threats. The best way to combat insider risks is to employ sound technological offerings, end-user education and policy enforcement across networks, says Ellen Libenson, vice president of product management at Symark, an identity management vendor.

"I think people are admitting to the fact that this is a pretty big problem. Unfortunately, it is a problem that if they institute best practices they could get rid of a lot of these instances," she says. "We like to think we can trust everyone around here, but we have these super users who can do the most harm. I'm not saying don't trust them, but it's the old Ronald Reagan thing: trust, but verify."

*"People are using the Internet to accomplish good, but sometimes with questionable means."*

# Vigilantism Motivates Some to Violate Cyber Laws

### Nancy Gohring

*In the following viewpoint, Nancy Gohring asserts that cyber vigilantes, taking the law into their own hands, illegally access personal computers to expose those they believe to be cyber criminals. She explains, for example, how a Canadian man used a Trojan horse—software that appears to perform one action while actually performing another—to uncover evidence of child pornography. Such actions are illegal because a vigilante hacker might unjustly accuse an innocent person with tragic consequences, she maintains. Gohring, a staff writer for IDG News Service, writes on high-tech subjects.*

As you read, consider the following questions:

1. What high-profile case put an end to Brad Willman's career as a cyber vigilante, according to Gohring?
2. What did Willman originally set out to do with his computer skills?

Nancy Gohring, "Crime and Punishment: Hacking for a Good Cause," *Computerworld*, December 31, 2007. Reproduced by permission.

3. What did Willman do after finding illicit documents or photos?

B rad Willman was installing networking equipment out of an emergency van in British Columbia when a policemen showed up and asked for him. Willman knew the officer from a case he was involved with a couple of years earlier, so he didn't worry—until he arrived at the police station and was introduced to a couple of U.S. cops.

The visit marked the end of Willman's version of vigilante justice.

## A Trojan Horse Used for Good

It was 2000, and Willman was 19. He had spent the last few years surreptitiously distributing a Trojan horse program to more than 1,000 people to try to uncover child-porn activities. All told, Willman said his work sent around seventy people to prison.

But then Willman stumbled on a prominent Californian judge. He discovered that Ronald Kline, at the time a superior court judge in Orange County, had a big collection of child porn and a diary on his PC indicating he was planning to try to seduce young boys. The high-profile case put an end to Willman's career as a crime-fighter.

"Oh, I knew it was illegal," Willman said in a recent phone interview. "But I really didn't care. I felt if I'm helping a few people in the process, cool." Until Kline, Willman had managed to stay anonymous.

## The Origins of the Program

Willman didn't initially set out to chase child pornographers. He started out developing a program designed to compete with pcAnywhere, Symantec's software that lets users access computers remotely.

## Who Should Impose Punishment?

A cybersecurity policy that condones both active deterrence and retaliation—without any judicial determination of wrong doing—is attractive, but it's wrongheaded, not least because it ignores the line between war, where those involved are permitted to determine when counterattack is required, and crime, where only impartial third parties (judges and juries) can impose punishment.

*Bruce Schneier,*
*"Vigilantism Is a Poor Response to Cyberattack,"*
*Wired, April 5, 2007.*

But then, while discussing programming on various newsgroups, he had a conversation with a Canadian man who offered his six-year-old daughter to Willman.

"That was an awkward scenario," Willman says, putting it mildly.

Willman quickly contacted the police, who were able to prosecute the Edmonton man, he said.

"He's more or less what altered my mind from competing with pcAnywhere to making a Trojan to see who else is doing this," he said.

Willman used the work he'd already developed on the program to trick suspected pedophiles into unknowingly downloading the software so that he could get proof from their computers.

Willman would visit child-porn newsgroups and post his program as a file that looked like it contained a photo. In order to avoid suspicion, Willman built in an additional feature. When the program launched without opening a photo, he designed it so that the first time it loaded it would display any photo from the directory to the user.

After someone downloaded the software, Willman could look through their files remotely for illicit documents or photos. Once he found damning information, he'd copy and share it with various child-porn watchdog groups, who could then pursue the perpetrators.

Everything changed when Kline downloaded the Trojan and Willman found damning evidence on the judge's computer.

Willman passed the information on to one of the watchdog groups as usual and figured that was that—until the day the police showed up while he was at work.

The police from the United States told him that they found him through correspondence sent from his computer to one of the watchdog groups.

While the police were initially friendly because Willman was able to give them additional information on Kline, they later told him that if he does any more hacking, ever, they'll arrest him. Willman signed an agreement that he wouldn't hack and that he wouldn't have anything to do with child porn.

## Legal Barriers to Vigilantism

Various state and federal laws in the United States criminalize unauthorized access to computers, said Jeff Neuburger, an attorney specializing in technology at Thelen Reid Brown Raysman & Steiner, an international law firm based in New York City. If Willman hadn't agreed to the deal with the police, he could have been charged with violating state or federal laws. But even in that case, so long as he didn't set foot in the United States., it would have been difficult for American authorities to prosecute him, Neuburger said.

He's seeing more and more cases like Willman's, where people are using the Internet to accomplish good, but sometimes with questionable means. "In the United States, prosecutors are careful not to let something like this go without sending a message that what the person did was wrong," he said. "But they may not aggressively seek a severe sentence or punishment."

One problem with vigilante work like Willman's is that someone might make a mistake and affect innocent people, Neuburger warned. Had Willman wrongly accused someone, he could have faced much bigger legal problems. "It's a dangerous thing," he said.

His days in the spotlight behind him, Willman, now twenty-seven, lives with his parents in Langley, B.C., where he does phone tech support for a small cable company. He does computer repair on the side and dreams of becoming a computer security researcher.

As for Kline, he was sentenced earlier this year to twenty-seven months in prison, a sentence that Willman called "reasonable."

Once in a while, Willman still gets a request from someone asking for his help in busting someone involved with child porn. He can only refer them to the watchdog groups he was familiar with.

"I would like to help these people get their kids in a better position, but I can't because the type of research I'd have to do is stuff I'm not allowed to do anymore," he said.

Even though Willman knew his actions were illegal, he didn't consider the consequences. "I thought I covered my tracks pretty well," he said. "And I did until the Judge Kline thing. I didn't really think I'd get busted."

> *"The explosive rise of Napster and P2P [peer-to-peer] was a form of civil unrest by consumers against an oppressive industry that had abused its customers."*

# Peer-to-Peer File-Sharing Is a Form of Rebellion Against Corporate Tyranny

*Marc Freedman*

*The following viewpoint was written in response to a July 9, 2003, Mi2N editorial, "THE BORG V. THE RIAA," by Eric de Fontenay, in which the author explores why file-sharing did not decline despite threats from the Recording Industry Association of America.*

In the following viewpoint, Marc Freeman argues that, despite threats from the Recording Industry Association of America (RIAA), consumers continue to download free music. The sharing of music, he asserts, is a form of rebellion against an oppressive music industry that maintains totalitarian control over music and the artists who create it. RIAA, Freedman claims, fixes prices, cheats artists, and uses its power to threaten its competition. *As long as RIAA continues these practices, consumers will continue to share free music, he claims. Freedman is founder of DiaRIAA, a Web site dedicated to opposing RIAA and helping artists and consumers.*

As you read, consider the following questions:

1. Why, in the author's view, is RIAA more powerful than a totalitarian government?
2. Who, in the author's view, are P2P users?
3. In the author's opinion, what has continued to fuel public outrage and P2P popularity?

Eric,

I admire your work but must disagree on this piece.

You ask "Who could have predicted it?" [that direct consumer litigation would INCREASE file-sharing]. Most anyone.

## A Totalitarian Regime

You accurately describe this consumer treatment "as a time-tested rule of extreme punishment . . . the cornerstone of more totalitarian regimes."

> *Totalitarian: Of relating to, being, or imposing a form of government in which the political authority exercises absolute and centralized control over all aspects of life, the individual is subordinated to the state, and opposing political and cultural expression is suppressed.*

Here's an industry that demands total control over its product and how its used, denies civil liberties to consumers, cloaks itself in its "moral imperative", threatens all businesses that oppose it, is convicted of price fixing and cheating artists, blatantly lies, and uses its massive power to pass one-sided legislation like the DMCA [Digital Millennium Copyright Act] (all documented at DiaRIAA.com). In fact, RIAA [Recording

## Artists Should Control Music

As the recording industry starts to lose control of how music is made and distributed, music will become more diversified. Formulaic music will not be as prevalent because it will cease to be as profitable as it once was, and the popularity of music will be defined by its innovation, not by virtue of the fact that it is backed by some major record label with deep pockets. . . .

Control of music needs to be given back to the artists and taken away from the corporations. Music is an art, and it should be shared with anyone who will listen.

*Jonathan Swihart,*
*"Fight the Power: Downloading to Empower Artists,"*
Campus Press *[University of Colorado], March 12, 2007.*

Industry Association of America] is better than a government. No one can vote RIAA off the island. In this drama, it is RIAA which pays the part of the relentless totalitarian Borg.

Do you truly expect Americans to drop the soap and submit to such an organization?

## Civil Unrest

We forget recent history all too quickly. The explosive rise of Napster and P2P [peer-to-peer] was a form of civil unrest by consumers against an oppressive industry that had abused its customers (such as charging MORE for CD's that cost LESS to produce) and refused to adapt to a digital realm that its customers already embraced.

This isn't about college kids, foreign CD pirates, or some fringe group. P2P users are not some irrational mob or collusive hive mind. There are 60 million U.S. P2P users. It's my daughter and her grandfather. This is the American public.

The market rules in our economy. And this market, the American public, was rebelling against the Borgian RIAA to fight for fairness, choice, and freedom. A rational reaction.

In response, RIAA proclaimed resistance was futile and brutally tried to maintain the status quo. It is RIAA that is acting irrationally, even silly at times, ignoring the public demands of the very market it needs to survive.

Over the past few years RIAA's behavior and the industry's lame online efforts have only continued to fuel public outrage and P2P popularity. Now RIAA's direct lawsuits scream into this same raw nerve. It's not difficult to predict that the public response will be the same as it's been the past five years. To vote with their time, software, bandwidth, and MP3 players on the side of P2P until the industry adapts. My money's on the Federation rebels.

I *"'The Internet is the ideal medium for terrorism today: anonymous but pervasive.'"*

# The Internet Helps Promote Terrorism

*Steve Coll and Susan B. Glasser*

*In the following viewpoint,* Washington Post *staff writers Steve Coll and Susan B. Glasser maintain that the anonymity and global reach of the Internet has helped facilitate terrorism. Internet terrorist recruits do not have to travel to terrorist camps to receive training, the authors assert. Terrorist recruits can access a vast online library of training resources that explain how to make bombs and plan attacks, the authors explain. Moreover, Coll and Glasser claim, the nature of the Internet makes thwarting terrorist attacks planned on the Internet more difficult than thwarting those planned in the physical world.*

As you read, consider the following questions:

1. According to Coll and Glasser, what cases have led Western intelligence agencies to believe that terrorism has become a "Web-directed" jihad movement?

2. In the authors' view, when are terrorists in the physical world most vulnerable?

3. What do the jihadist cyberworld and other digital communities have in common, in the authors' opinion?

In the snow-draped mountains near Jalalabad, [Afghanistan] in November 2001, as the Taliban collapsed and al Qaeda lost its Afghan sanctuary, Osama bin Laden biographer Hamid Mir watched "every second al Qaeda member carrying a laptop computer along with a Kalashnikov [an AK-47]" as they prepared to scatter into hiding and exile. On the screens were photographs of Sept. 11, [2001, terrorist attack] hijacker Mohamed Atta.

## Migrating to Cyberspace

Nearly four years later, al Qaeda has become the first guerrilla movement in history to migrate from physical space to cyberspace. With laptops and DVDs, in secret hideouts and at neighborhood Internet cafes, young code-writing jihadists have sought to replicate the training, communication, planning and preaching facilities they lost in Afghanistan with countless new locations on the Internet.

Al Qaeda suicide bombers and ambush units in Iraq routinely depend on the Web for training and tactical support, relying on the Internet's anonymity and flexibility to operate with near impunity in cyberspace. In Qatar, Egypt and Europe, cells affiliated with al Qaeda that have recently carried out or seriously planned bombings have relied heavily on the Internet.

Such cases have led Western intelligence agencies and outside terrorism specialists to conclude that the "global jihad movement," sometimes led by al Qaeda fugitives but increasingly made up of diverse "groups and ad hoc cells," has become a "Web-directed" phenomenon, as a presentation for U.S. government terrorism analysts by longtime State Depart-

ment expert Dennis Pluchinsky put it. Hampered by the nature of the Internet itself, the government has proven ineffective at blocking or even hindering significantly this vast online presence.

## An Online Training Library

Among other things, al Qaeda and its offshoots are building a massive and dynamic online library of training materials—some supported by experts who answer questions on message boards or in chat rooms—covering such varied subjects as how to mix ricin poison, how to make a bomb from commercial chemicals, how to pose as a fisherman and sneak through Syria into Iraq, how to shoot at a U.S. soldier, and how to navigate by the stars while running through a night-shrouded desert. These materials are cascading across the Web in Arabic, Urdu, Pashto and other first languages of jihadist volunteers.

The Saudi Arabian branch of al Qaeda launched an online magazine in 2004 that exhorted potential recruits to use the Internet: "Oh Mujahid brother, in order to join the great training camps you don't have to travel to other lands," declared the inaugural issue of Muaskar al-Battar, or Camp of the Sword. "Alone, in your home or with a group of your brothers, you too can begin to execute the training program."

"Biological Weapons" was the stark title of a fifteen-page Arabic language document posted two months ago on the Web site of al Qaeda fugitive leader Mustafa Setmariam Nasar, one of the jihadist movement's most important propagandists, often referred to by the nom de guerre Abu Musab Suri. His document described "how the pneumonic plague could be made into a biological weapon," if a small supply of the virus could be acquired, according to a translation by Rebecca Givner-Forbes, an analyst at the Terrorism Research Center, an Arlington [Virginia] firm with U.S. government clients. Nasar's guide drew on U.S. and Japanese biological weapons programs

from the World War II era and showed "how to inject carrier animals, like rats, with the virus and how to extract microbes from infected blood . . . and how to dry them so that they can be used with an aerosol delivery system."

## Overcoming Obstacles in the Physical World

Jihadists seek to overcome in cyberspace specific obstacles they face from armies and police forces in the physical world. In planning attacks, radical operatives are often at risk when they congregate at a mosque or cross a border with false documents. They are safer working on the Web. Al Qaeda and its offshoots "have understood that both time and space have in many ways been conquered by the Internet," said John Arquilla, a professor at the Naval Postgraduate School who coined the term "netwar" more than a decade ago.

Al Qaeda's innovation on the Web "erodes the ability of our security services to hit them when they're most vulnerable, when they're moving," said Michael Scheuer, former chief of the CIA unit that tracked bin Laden. "It used to be they had to go to Sudan, they had to go to Yemen, they had to go to Afghanistan to train," he added. Now, even when such travel is necessary, an al Qaeda operative "no longer has to carry anything that's incriminating. He doesn't need his schematics, he doesn't need his blueprints, he doesn't need formulas." Everything is posted on the Web or "can be sent ahead by encrypted Internet, and it gets lost in the billions of messages that are out there."

The number of active jihadist-related Web sites has metastasized since Sept. 11, 2001. When Gabriel Weimann, a professor at the University of Haifa in Israel, began tracking terrorist-related Web sites eight years ago, he found twelve; today, he tracks more than 4,500. Hundreds of them celebrate al Qaeda or its ideas, he said.

## Why Cyberterror?

Why would terrorists turn to cyberterrorism? Because it has certain advantages over the traditional physical methods of terrorist attacks. The Internet is the instrument of a political power shift. A many-to-many communication system, the Internet is cheap, relatively safe (doesn't require any dangerous handling of explosive materials) and secretive (not even revealing the terrorist's location or identity). A cyberterror attack can be conducted from almost any locale in the world and is capable of worldwide impact. It's been hypothesized that the new, modern cyberterrorist can do more damage via the internet than with a bomb.

*D E Levine,*
*"Cyberterrorrism: Welcome to the Front Lines,"*
Security Technology & Design, *April 2006.*

## A Virtual Community

"They are all linked indirectly through association of belief, belonging to some community. The Internet is the network that connects them all," Weimann said. "You can see the virtual community come alive."

Apart from its ideology and clandestine nature, the jihadist cyberworld is little different in structure from digital communities of role-playing gamers, eBay coin collectors or disease sufferers. Through continuous online contact, such communities bind dispersed individuals with intense beliefs who might never have met one another in the past. Along with radical jihad, the Internet also has enabled the flow of powerful ideas and inspiration in many other directions, such as encouraging democratic movements and creating vast new commercial markets.

Since the U.S. invasion of Iraq more than two years ago, the Web's growth as a jihadist meeting and training ground has accelerated.

But al Qaeda's move into cyberspace is far from total. Physical sanctuaries or unmolested spaces in Sunni Muslim-dominated areas of Iraq, in ungoverned tribal territories of Pakistan, in the southern Philippines, Africa and Europe still play important roles. Most violent al Qaeda-related attacks—even in the most recent period of heavy jihadist Web use—appear to involve leaders or volunteers with some traditional training camp or radical mosque backgrounds.

But the Web's growing centrality in al Qaeda-related operations and incitement has led such analysts as former CIA deputy director John E. McLaughlin to describe the movement as primarily driven today by "ideology and the Internet."

The Web's shapeless disregard for national boundaries and ethnic markers fits exactly with bin Laden's original vision for al Qaeda, which he founded to stimulate revolt among the worldwide Muslim *ummah*, or community of believers. Bin Laden's appeal among some Muslims has long flowed in part from his rare willingness among Arab leaders to surround himself with racially and ethnically diverse followers, to ignore ancient prejudices and national borders. In this sense of utopian ambition, the Web has become a gathering place for a rainbow coalition of jihadists. It offers al Qaeda "a virtual sanctuary" on a global scale, Rand Corp. terrorism specialist Bruce Hoffman said. "The Internet is the ideal medium for terrorism today: anonymous but pervasive."

## Adapting to Technology

In Afghanistan, the Taliban banned television and even toothbrushes as forbidden modern innovations. Yet al Qaeda, led by educated and privileged gadget hounds, adapted early and enthusiastically to the technologies of globalization, and its Arab volunteers managed to evade the Taliban's screen-smashing technology police.

Bin Laden used some of the first commercial satellite telephones while hiding out in Afghanistan. He produced propaganda videos with hand-held cameras long before the genre became commonplace. Bin Laden's sons played computer games in their compound in Jalalabad, recalled the journalist Abdel Bari Atwan, who interviewed bin Laden late in 1996.

Today, however, bin Laden and his deputy, Ayman Zawahiri, have fallen well behind their younger followers worldwide. The two still make speeches that must be recorded in a makeshift studio and couriered at considerable risk to al-Jazeera or other satellite stations.... Their younger adherents have moved on to Web sites and the production of short videos with shock appeal that can be distributed to millions instantly via the Internet.

Many online videos seek to replicate the Afghan training experience. An al Qaeda video library discovered on the Web and obtained by The *Washington Post* from an experienced researcher showed in a series of high-quality training films shot in Afghanistan how to conduct a roadside assassination, raid a house, shoot a rocket-propelled grenade, blow up a car, attack a village, destroy a bridge and fire an SA-7 surface-to-air missile. During a practice hostage-taking, the filmmakers chuckled as trainees herded men and women into a room, screaming in English, "Move! Move!"

One of al Qaeda's current Internet organizations, the Global Islamic Media Front, is now posting "a lot of training materials that we've been able to verify were used in Afghanistan," said Givner-Forbes, of the Terrorism Research Center. One recent online manual instructed how to extract explosive materials from missiles and land mines. Another offered a country-by-country list of "explosive materials available in Western markets," including France, Germany, Italy, Japan, the former Soviet Union and Britain.

These sites have converted sections of the Web into "an open university for jihad," said Reuven Paz, who heads the

Project for the Research of Islamist Movements in Israel. "The main audience is the younger generation in the Arab world" who now can peruse at their own pace "one big *madrạssa* on the Internet." . . .

Until recently, al Qaeda's use of the Web appeared to be centered on communications: preaching, recruitment, community-building and broad incitement. But there is increasing evidence that al Qaeda and its offshoots are also using the Internet for tactical purposes, especially for training new adherents. "If you want to conduct an attack, you will find what you need on the Internet," said Rita Katz, director of the SITE Institute, a group that monitors and tracks the jihadist Internet sites. . . .

## Protecting Secret Communications

The movement has also innovated with great creativity to protect its most secret communications. Khalid Sheik Mohammed, a key planner of the Sept. 11 attacks later arrested in Pakistan, used what four researchers familiar with the technique called an electronic or virtual "dead drop" on the Web to avoid having his e-mails intercepted by eavesdroppers in the United States or allied governments. Mohammed or his operatives would open an account on a free, public e-mail service such as Hotmail, write a message in draft form, save it as a draft, then transmit the e-mail account name and password during chatter on a relatively secure message board, according to these researchers.

The intended recipient could then open the e-mail account and read the draft—since no e-mail message was sent, there was a reduced risk of interception, the researchers said.

Matt Devost, president of the Terrorism Research Center, who has done research in the field for a decade, recalled that "silverbullet" was one of the passwords Mohammed reportedly used in this period. Sending fake streams of e-mail spam to disguise a single targeted message is another innovation used by jihadist communicators, specialists said.

Al Qaeda's success with such tactics has underscored the difficulty of gathering intelligence against the movement. Mohammed's e-mails, once discovered, "were the best actionable intelligence in the whole war" against bin Laden and his adherents, said Arquilla, the Naval Postgraduate School professor. But al Qaeda has been keenly aware of its electronic pursuers and has tried to do what it can to stay ahead—mostly by using encryption.

In the last two years, a small number of cases have emerged in which jihadist cells appear to have formed among like-minded strangers who met online, according to intelligence officials and terrorism specialists. And there are many other cases in which bonds formed in the physical world have been sustained and nurtured by the Internet, according to specialists in and outside of government.

> *"Many of the attributes of [Internet] technology—low cost, ease of use, accessibility, anonymous nature, among others—make it an attractive medium for a new reality known as 'cyberstalking.'"*

# Stalkers Use the Internet to Pursue Their Victims

*Kacy Silverstein*

*In the following viewpoint, Kacy Silverstein claims that easy accessibility and anonymity make the Internet an effective new way for stalkers to abuse their victims. Stalkers can prowl the Web unobserved to threaten and discredit their targets, she asserts. While stalkers in the physical world often have some prior connection to their victims, the Internet is making stranger stalking more common, Silverstein maintains. She reasons that the nationwide reach of the Internet and the maze of state cyberstalking laws make clear the need for a standard federal law. Silverstein is associate director for Project Safe, a sexual and domestic violence program at Vanderbilt University.*

Kacy Silverstein, "Cyberstalking: Understanding Stalker's Virtual Frontier," *Inside Vandy*, January 17, 2007. Copyright © 2008 Vanderbilt Student Communications, Inc. Reproduced by permission.

As you read, consider the following questions:

1. How does the U.S. Department of Justice define cyber-stalking?

2. In Silverstein's opinion, what motivates someone to chase someone down the information superhighway?

3. What is the key to a successful cyber-stalking prosecution, in the author's view?

A fairly new reality may lurk in a place you least expect it: your computer. We crossed into the new millennium with a rapidly growing information superhighway, improving our ability to connect with others at almost every corner of the globe. The Internet is advancing our connection to friends and family, improving education, and promoting discussion and dialogue with people from across the street to across the world. Unfortunately, many of the attributes of [Internet] technology—low cost, ease of use, accessibility, anonymous nature, among others—make it an attractive medium for a new reality known as "cyberstalking." Although there is no universally accepted definition of cyberstalking, the U.S. Department of Justice defines it as "the uses of Internet, e-mail, and other electronic communications devices to stalk another person". While cyberstalking may not involve physical contact with the victim, unlike other types of stalking, it is fundamentally an extension of its terrestrial cousin. Many stalkers, whether in virtual reality or physical reality, are motivated by a desire to exert control over the victims and engage in similar types of behavior to accomplish this end. As with other types of stalking, the majority of perpetrators are men and the majority of their victims are women, although there have been reported cases of women cyberstalking men and same-sex cyberstalking.

## The Scope of Cyberstalking

So, with the Internet providing new avenues for stalkers to pursue victims by a few clicks of the mouse or keystrokes,

how does this alter the physical and virtual landscape of stalking? Victim service providers report that the "Internet is rapidly becoming another weapon used by batterers against their victims. Just as in real life, abused women can be followed in cyberspace by their batterers, who may surreptitiously place their target under surveillance without her knowledge and use the information to threaten her or discredit her." Cyberstalkers can take advantage of the impersonal, non-confrontational, and anonymous nature of the Web, sending harassing or threatening messages by the simple push of a button. More sophisticated cyber prowlers use programs to send messages to victims at regular or random intervals, even going so far as to post controversial messages in Internet chat rooms or on "revenge" bulletin boards. With minimal effort and possibly total anonymity, cyberstalkers are navigating a whole new arena where intellect and tech-skills replace body and brawn to frighten and intimidate victims. While the majority of cyberstalkers reported to law enforcement and WHOA (Working to Halt Online Abuse) appear to know their victim either through past romantic or platonic relationships, stalkers with no prior connection to victims are taking advantage of emerging technologies. Jayne Hitchcock, president of Working to Halt Online Abuse explains, "for the cases where the victim knows their harasser, it's usually revenge. For the stranger-on-stranger cases, it's most often what I call 'Internet road rage.' What is it that causes a person to chase someone down a highway offline? The same goes for the superhighway—it could be something as simple as the harasser not liking the victim's username to a perceived injustice to not liking what someone posted online." While cyberstalking continues to gain the attention of the media and technology experts, there is very little empirical evidence upon which to estimate its actual magnitude. It has been argued, however, that cyberstalking may actually be more common than more traditional forms of stalking. This is because the Internet, as a medium of com-

## Why Do People Cyberstalk or Cyberharass Others?

Cyberstalkers are often driven by revenge, hate, anger, jealousy, obsession, and mental illness. While a cyberharasser may be motivated by some of these same feelings, often the harassment is driven by the desire to frighten or embarrass the harassment victim. Sometimes the harasser intends to teach the victim a lesson in netiquette or political correctness (from the harasser's point of view). Often the cyberharassment victim is merely in the wrong place at the wrong time, or has made a comment or expressed an opinion that the cyberharasser dislikes. We've even seen cases where the victim is being targeted because they're the first ones the cyberharasser encounters when they are in a "bad mood."

*Parry Aftab,*
*"Understanding the Cyberharassment Problem,"*
Information Week, *August 23, 2006.*

munication, allows cyberstalkers immense contact with potential victims. "We don't see cyberstalking going away," explains Jayne Hitchcock. "In fact, it is increasing every day. Currently there are over one billion people online worldwide—if one percent become victims, that's ten million people."

## No Clearly Defined Law

Now that many of us have made the Internet a home within the home and cyberstalkers prowl anonymously and with ease, where does the law stand? At the current time, no uniform-federal laws exist regarding cyberstalking. Federal law does provide a number of important tools that are valuable to combat cyberstalking, including eighteen U.S.C. 875 (c) "making it a federal crime punishable by up to five years in prison

and a fine of up to \$250,000, to transmit any communication in interstate or foreign commerce containing a threat to injure the person or another." Nonetheless, the absence of a clearly defined cyberstalking law at the federal level has forced some states to draft their own specific legislation. As a result, potential victims are often faced with a complicated maze of laws offering varying definitions, protections, and penalties. At last count, forty-five states had laws expressly prohibiting harassing conduct through the Internet, e-mail, or other electronic means. Tennessee state law regarding stalking was amended in 2002 to include electronic communication, electronic email, or Internet services. As many state stalking laws have been adapted to either explicitly or implicitly include cyberstalking statutes, it is often difficult for law enforcement to get involved. Until a uniform federal standard exists, the best source for cyberstalking guidance is states with current legislation on the subject. In most cases, taking into account varying state and federal standards, the key to a successful cyberstalking prosecution is to preserve a full electronic trail of evidence. A growing number of law enforcement agencies are recognizing the serious nature and extent of cyberstalking and responding with aggressive action. In larger cities, such as New York and Los Angeles, specialized units have been developed to ensure that special sections of police departments and district attorney's offices are available when cyberstalking cases arise. As the information superhighway continues to evolve, law enforcement at all levels must become more sensitive to cyberstalking and its nuances.

## Combating Cyberstalking

As cyberstalking is expected to increase as computers and the Internet become more popular and easily accessible, how do we combat this crime? A critical step in combating cyberstalking is an understanding of stalking in general. In many instances, "cyberstalking is simply another phase in an overall

stalking pattern, or it is regular stalking behavior using new, high-technology tools." Because cyberstalking is a relatively new criminal phenomenon complicated by Internet anonymity and lack of resources to address the crime, victims of online harassment and threats have had to develop their own informal support networks and informational Web sites. Victim service providers recommend that victims make copies of all electronic communications sent by the cyberstalker as evidence of his stalking and advise a victim to let the stalker know that she does not want any further contact with him. In addition, it is important that we all name the behavior as cyberstalking and validate that a crime is occurring when working with victims.

Similar to other forms of violence against women, cyberstalking is a serious crime that is often underreported and lacking public attention. Yet, computers and the Internet are now indispensable parts of American culture and it is not enough to just "turn off your computer." We must all become more sensitive to the fear and frustration experienced by cyberstalking victims and aware that cyberstalking is in many ways simply an extension of other forms of violence against women.

# Periodical Bibliography

*The following articles have been selected to supplement the diverse views presented in this chapter.*

| | |
|---|---|
| Benjamin Cohen | "Policing the Internet Requires Understanding of How It Works," *New Media Age*, September 22, 2005. |
| Joris Evers | "Online Threats Outpacing Law Crackdowns," *C/Net News*, June 15, 2006. |
| *eWeek* | "Symantec: Profit Drive Cyber-Crime Won't Stop," November 17, 2006. |
| Chad Jimenez | "A Pirate's Life for Me," *Claremont Independent*, December 12, 2007. |
| Brian Krebs | "Cyber Crime 2.0; In 2007, Online Fraud Got More Targeted and Sophisticated," *Washington Post*, December 20, 2007. |
| Peter Lewis | "Hackers Get Bum Rap for Corporate America's Digital Delinquency," *UW News*, March 13, 2007. |
| Calum Macleod | "EXPOSED! Top Hacker Secrets . . . ," *Management Services*, Summer 2007. |
| Douglas S. Malan | "Intimidation Goes Online (cyberbullying)," *Connecticut Law Tribune*, December 24, 2007. |
| Bruce Schneier | "Vigilantism Is a Poor Response to Cyberattack," *Wired*, April 5, 2007. |
| Jonathan Swihart | "Fight the Power: Downloading to Empower Artists," *Campus Press [University of Colorado]*, March 12, 2007. |
| Breanne Wagner | "Electronic Attackers," *National Defense*, October 2007. |

# How Can Companies and Consumers Reduce the Impact of Cyber Crime?

# Chapter Preface

Many believe that information is power. Indeed, the sale of personal information has become big business. The Fair Credit Reporting Act of 1970 gave credit-reporting companies the right to sell "credit headers" to lenders and mortgage brokers. Credit headers provide information such as names, addresses, job information, birthdates, phone numbers, and Social Security numbers about consumers. Armed with this information, the credit industry began to bombard consumers with credit card offers, and the credit industry blossomed. "In 1970 . . . just one in six Americans possessed a [credit] card. Today, three in four carry cards," claims consumer policy analyst Robert Hahn. Seeing the enormous potential of consumer information, large data brokerage firms soon emerged. These firms acquire consumer data from public records and sort, analyze, and sell it. When some of the large data brokerage firms and institutions were invaded by data thieves in 2005, consumer advocates began to look for ways to protect consumers. One strategy—to compel data brokers to obtain consumer permission before selling information—remains hotly contested as one of several controversies in the debate over how to best respond to the threat of cyber crime. Consumer rights advocates argue that requiring data collection companies to ask permission before selling consumer information will reduce identity theft. The business community claims, however, that such a requirement restricts the credit market, which is not good for consumers or creditors.

Those who claim that data brokers should obtain consumer permission before selling personal information argue that consumer-information policies must make personal information less valuable. According to security expert Bruce Schneier, if information were harder to get, it would be less

valuable, and therefore, less appealing to those hoping to use it to commit fraud. "Financial services needs to slow down and take security more seriously," Schneier asserts. He maintains that Europe, where identity theft is less of a problem, is a good model. Senator Byron Dorgan agrees. "The Europeans require companies to provide consumers with notice, the ability to opt out with respect to non-sensitive commercial marketing of personal information, opt in with respect to sensitive personal information, the right of access to personal information collected, [and] reasonable security protections for the information," Dorgan maintains.

Those who oppose consumer preauthorization of the sale of personal data argue that such a policy would restrict the credit market. "There is a role for information in creating a more competitive marketplace by letting new parties enter the market," argues Martin Abrams, executive director for the Center for Information Policy Leadership. "I believe the opportunity created there counterbalances the privacy gain," Abrams observes. Opponents of consumer preauthorization also fear that restrictions will make it easier for identity thieves. "If [restrictions go] too far," claims LexisNexis' Hurt Sanford, "we will, in fact, enable the bad guys to do even more than they're doing now." According to Sanford, broad restrictions might inhibit access to data that law enforcement personnel need to hunt down identity thieves.

Whether consumer preauthorization of the sale of personal information would benefit or hurt the consumer remains the subject of rigorous debate. The authors in the following chapter present their opinions about how companies and consumers can best reduce the impact of cyber crime.

| *"The right to freeze one's credit ought to be legally guaranteed nationwide."*

# Consumers Should Be Allowed to Freeze Their Credit History

### Anita Ramasastry

*In the following viewpoint, Anita Ramasastry argues that consumers vulnerable to identity theft should be guaranteed the right to freeze their credit. While warning victims and pursuing perpetrators are important tools, the best way to protect consumers is to allow them to freeze their credit and prevent identity thieves from opening new accounts or obtaining credit in the first place, Ramasastry reasons. She maintains that concerns about the impact of delayed access to credit should not prevent freezes; such concerns should encourage policy makers to make rules that prevent delays. Ramasastry is an associate professor at the University of Washington School of Law.*

As you read, consider the following questions:

1. According to the Federal Trade Commission, how did ChoicePoint violate federal consumer protection laws?

2. In Ramasastry's opinion, why have remedies to identity theft been ineffective thus far?

Anita Ramasastry, "Whose Credit Report Is It, Anyway? It's Time for States to Pass Credit Freeze Laws That Give Consumers Control Over Their Credit Profiles," *FindLaw Writ*, February 6, 2006. Reproduced by permission.

3. What are some of the features of state credit freeze laws, according to the author?

In late January [2006], the Federal Trade Commission (FTC) announced that data broker ChoicePoint will pay $10 million to the commission, and $5 million to redress consumer harms caused by a large data breach. It is reportedly the largest civil penalty in FTC history.

According to the FTC, ChoicePoint sold records of at least 163,000 individuals to a criminal ring of identity thieves—and thereby violated federal consumer protection laws. It did so, the FTC says, by failing to maintain reasonable procedures to protect consumer data, and also by falsely advertising that it adequately shielded personal information from fraud and misuse.

Thus far, ChoicePoint's sale of personal data to thieves has caused at least 800 consumers to fall prey to identity theft. It can take months or years to repair one's credit history once this happens.

What, if anything, can consumers do to protect themselves from such breaches—which are only becoming more commonplace? Recently, state legislatures have begun to examine an important new protective measure—credit report "freezes."

In this column, I'll explain how the freezes work, and argue that the right to freeze one's credit ought to be legally guaranteed nationwide.

## The Status Quo

Identity theft is a growing problem. When impostors assume the identity of innocent consumers—by gaining access, from companies, to sensitive consumer data such as Social Security numbers, dates of birth, mother's maiden names, bank account numbers, and more—they can make purchases on credit, and potentially destroy the consumer's credit history.

Thus far, remedies have proved largely ineffective. Victims are told to try to shield their personal information from loss

or theft—but how can they, when they must give certain identifying information to companies with which they deal? Also, while criminal penalties for identity theft have been heightened, impostors still may evade detection, and even if they are caught, their victim's credit history is still destroyed.

Warning victims and jailing impostors—if they are caught—is not enough. It's time to focus on the companies that hold data, and those that maintain credit reports, too.

For instance, some critics of the current system point out that if merchants and credit-granting institutions weren't so lax in granting credit in the first place, then impostors would find it much more difficult to succeed.

The pressures of market competition seem to be to blame for the ease of getting credit, even fraudulently: If one company has strict credit practices, another company with laxer practices will beat the first company in the market. Yet the market as a whole would benefit from stricter practices, for companies currently must write off the sums impostors steal.

## The Virtues of the Right to "Freeze"

Other critics—such as privacy advocate Chris Hoofnagle—argue that customers ought to be able to command companies to "freeze" their credit reports with the major credit reporting bureaus.

This right to freeze one's credit history, it is argued, ought to be triggered as soon as suspicious activity occurs—such as the theft of a purse, of mail from a financial company, or of a credit card—*before*, identity theft can occur. The result of the freeze would be simple: Identity thieves would not be able to open new credit accounts or obtain credit easily.

After the freeze, advocates explain, a consumer could "thaw" his or her file, but only partially, specifying to whom, when, or in what circumstances information should be released.

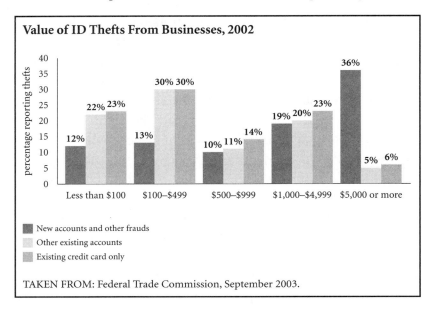

**Value of ID Thefts From Businesses, 2002**

New accounts and other frauds

Other existing accounts

Existing credit card only

TAKEN FROM: Federal Trade Commission, September 2003.

In the beginning of 2005, only four states had credit freeze laws on the books: California and Louisiana, for all consumers; and Texas and Vermont, for identity theft victims only.

At the start of 2006, twelve states in total had such legislation. Now, however, twenty-seven states are considering security freeze bills—including California and Texas, which have filed bills to expand their existing security freeze laws.[1]

Such laws typically have the following definitions, and features:

A consumer must request a freeze in writing and must provide a valid police report showing either identity theft, or the kind of theft (as of a purse or credit card) that leads to identity theft. A "freeze" consists of a notice placed on that person's credit report, at the person's request. It prohibits

1. As of March 2008, thirty-nine states and the District of Columbia have enacted laws requiring the credit bureaus—Equifax, Experian, and TransUnion—to enable consumers to protect their credit files with a security freeze. On November 1, 2007, the three credit bureaus voluntarily offered the security freeze to consumers living in the eleven states that have not yet adopted security freeze laws freeze and also to consumers in the four states with laws that limit this protection to identity theft victims only.

consumer-reporting agencies from releasing the credit report without express authorization by the consumer.

Normally, the freeze remains in effect until the consumer asks for it to be removed. But the freeze can be lifted if the consumer materially misrepresents the relevant facts.

As noted above, some states extend the right to freeze a credit report to *all*, consumers, including those who only *suspect* they will soon be identity theft victims. But others extend the right only to *actual* identity theft victims. (For instance, Washington State defines an identity theft victim for these purposes, as one whose identification or other personal information has been used with the intent to commit, or to aid or abet, any crime.)

Most of the laws apply to "credit reports" but a few states have enacted provisions applying more broadly to "consumer reports"—encompassing virtually any report that could be utilized by insurers for underwriting and fraud prevention, including insurance claims histories.

## The Criticisms of "Credit Freeze" Laws

Critics of "credit freeze" laws complain that it will take too long to lift a credit freeze—from several to as many as twelve days in some cases. They fear that freezes, especially if they linger too long, could lead to reduced consumer sales (especially on credit) and an overall economic downturn. It's for this reason many businesses have joined forces with credit granting institutions, spending millions of dollars on lobbying against credit freeze legislation.

Consumers, too, may be affected if freezes take too long to lift—especially if they need to, for instance, purchase auto insurance or a major appliance (on credit) right away. But these delays aren't, in my view, a reason to junk credit freeze laws: They're simply a reason to expedite the lifting of freezes.

For instance, in Utah, one proposed bill would allow the consumer to lift a credit freeze for a merchant of their choos-

ing on only fifteen minutes notice—simply by calling the credit bureau, and providing some personal information and a PIN number.

The fact that states—which doubtless will experiment with different approaches—are still working out the kinks in figuring out how freezes can be expeditiously lifted, does not mean that freeze laws are a bad idea. Remember, both consumers and businesses lose when freezes are not possible—for consumers are victimized by identity theft that can take years to correct, and businesses typically must cover the thefts out of their own pockets.

## A Federal Minimum Standard

Of course, a credit freeze law can only prevent fraud if consumers use it. And they will only use it, if it is designed to be user-friendly: free of charge, easy to initiate, quick to take effect, and easy to lift.

It's best if the various states fulfill their role as "laboratories" when it comes to the laws in this area. Perhaps Congress should state the minimum a state must do—for instance, that it must legally allow a credit freed once identity theft has been proven. But states should be able to figure out what they think is the best solution—looking to each other's laws as possible models.

The alternative is giving up—and giving in to the identity thieves. Surely, there's a better solution.

| "Consumers will see for themselves that a credit-file freeze is tantamount to freezing themselves out of the marketplace."

# Consumers Should Not Be Allowed to Freeze Their Credit History

*Stuart Pratt*

*In the following viewpoint, Stuart Pratt maintains that giving consumers the right to freeze their credit does more to punish them than it does to protect them. Consumers with frozen credit will find it difficult to unfreeze their credit when they need to buy a home or a car, he asserts. Moreover, Pratt claims, consumers will have to keep track of multiple pin numbers and protect these numbers from identity thieves. Policy makers should put current identity theft protections to the test before passing new, untested laws, he reasons. Pratt is president and CEO of the Consumer Data Industry Association.*

As you read, consider the following questions:

1. In Pratt's opinion, what can stop a credit application in its tracks?

Stuart Pratt, "Should Consumers Be Allowed to 'Freeze' Their Credit Histories?" *CQ Researcher*, June 10, 2005. Reproduced by permission.

2. What amendments to the Fair Credit Reporting Act does the author believe will create lender accountability?

3. What does the author argue should be the emphasis when targeting identity theft?

What sounds like a good idea is, in reality, a failure to apply the practical to the way we all expect to live our lives. The fact is, we want to be able to apply for credit, refinance our homes, buy new cars, start small businesses, and send our kids to college. In every one of these cases we want to take advantage of the best price when it is offered, and we don't want rigid rules to stop an application cold in its tracks.

Now, this isn't to say that speed is everything or is the only priority. Consumers expect and tolerate extra steps taken to verify identities, and they expect lenders to be careful about processing an application.

A new law that became effective Dec. 1, 2004, requires lenders to take additional steps to avoid identity [ID] theft and credit fraud. By having lenders verify identities, reconcile address variances and contact consumers where there are fraud alerts on file, these amendments to the Fair Credit Reporting Act created the accountability that consumers expect to be applied in every transaction. Consumers will benefit from these new rights and duties imposed on lenders and consumer-reporting agencies.

## Penalizing, Not Protecting Consumers

File freezing is not the answer, as has been shown in states that have such a law. We should all be dubious of legislation that will ostensibly protect us but really ends up penalizing us by imposing rigid rules.

Consumers will realize that they don't know which report to freeze or unfreeze, and they will experience how difficult it is to open up a file at just the right time for just the right transaction. Consumers also will experience the difficulty of

## Unintended Consequences

Allowing people to block creditors from viewing their credit histories is seen by well-meaning state legislators as a way to protect the privacy of their residents and guard against identity theft. But officials of the National Association of Mortgage Brokers warned . . . that so-called credit-freeze laws could backfire because their members will be unable to generate credit scores for their clients.

*Lew Sichelman,*
*"New Credit-Freeze Laws Could Backfire,"*
San Francisco Chronicle, *July 17, 2005.*

maintaining multiple PIN numbers (and protecting them from ID theft), which cannot be used on the spot at a mortgage broker's or auto dealer's office to unfreeze their credit reports.

In short, consumers will see for themselves that a credit-file freeze is tantamount to freezing themselves out of the marketplace, and they will not be able to take advantage of the deals it offers to consumers.

Congress passed sweeping identity-theft legislation two years ago. We believe that the new federal provisions targeting ID theft should be given a chance to make an impact before passing additional legislation. The emphasis should be on enforcing existing law, prosecuting criminals and educating consumers on how to prevent and spot credit-fraud risks, rather than creating additional legislation.

"*It's the software manufacturers that should be held liable, not the individual programmers.*"

# Software Manufacturers Should Be Liable for Internet Security Breaches

*Bruce Schneier*

*In the following viewpoint, Bruce Schneier contends that holding software manufacturers liable for security breaches in the software that they develop will lead to improvements in software security. Currently, the cost of insecure software is borne by the consumer who in many cases is not qualified to distinguish whether software is secure and insecure, Schneier maintains. If manufacturers bore the costs of software insecurity, they would be more likely to develop secure software, he reasons. Schneier is CTO of Counterpane Internet Security and the author of* Beyond Fear: Thinking Sensible About Security in an Uncertain World.

As you read, consider the following questions:

1. In Schneier's view, what are the costs of secure and insecure software that companies try to balance?

Bruce Schneier, "Sue Companies, Not Coders," *Wired*, October 20, 2005. Reproduced by permission.

2. In the author's opinion, why is it hard for the average buyer to distinguish a truly secure from an insecure product?

3. What extra costs are users already paying for insecure software, in the author's opinion?

At a security conference last week, Howard Schmidt, the former White House cybersecurity adviser, took the bold step of arguing that software developers should be held personally accountable for the security of the code they write.

He's on the right track, but he's made a dangerous mistake. It's the software manufacturers that should be held liable, not the individual programmers. Getting this one right will result in more-secure software for everyone; getting it wrong will simply result in a lot of messy lawsuits.

## Understanding Economic Incentives

To understand the difference, it's necessary to understand the basic economic incentives of companies, and how businesses are affected by liabilities. In a capitalist society, businesses are profit-making ventures, and they make decisions based on both short- and long-term profitability. They try to balance the costs of more-secure software—extra developers, fewer features, longer time to market—against the costs of insecure software: expense to patch, occasional bad press, potential loss of sales.

The result is what you see all around you: lousy software. Companies find that it's cheaper to weather the occasional press storm, spend money on PR campaigns touting good security, and fix public problems after the fact than to design security right from the beginning.

The problem with this analysis is that most of the costs of insecure software fall on the users. In economics, this is known as an externality: an effect of a decision not borne by the decision maker.

Normally, you would expect users to respond by favoring secure products over insecure products—after all, they're making their own buying decisions based on the same capitalist model. But that's not generally possible. In some cases, software monopolies limit the available product choice; in other cases, the "lock-in effect" created by proprietary file formats or existing infrastructure or compatibility requirements makes it harder to switch; and in still other cases, none of the competing companies have made security a differentiating characteristic. In all cases, it's hard for an average buyer to distinguish a truly secure product from an insecure product with a "boy, are we secure" marketing campaign.

The end result is that insecure software is common. But because users, not software manufacturers, pay the price, nothing improves. Making software manufacturers liable fixes this externality.

## Making Manufacturers Pay for Poor Software

Watch the mechanism work. If end users can sue software manufacturers for product defects, then the cost of those defects to the software manufacturers rises. Manufacturers are now paying the true economic cost for poor software, and not just a piece of it. So when they're balancing the cost of making their software secure versus the cost of leaving their software insecure, there are more costs on the latter side. This will provide an incentive for them to make their software more secure.

To be sure, making software more secure will cost money, and manufacturers will have to pass those costs on to users in the form of higher prices. But users are already paying extra costs for insecure software: costs of third-party security products, costs of consultants and security-services companies, direct and indirect costs of losses. Making software manufacturers liable moves those costs around, and as a byproduct causes the quality of software to improve.

This is why Schmidt's idea won't work. He wants individual software developers to be liable, and not the corporations. This will certainly give pissed-off users someone to sue, but it won't reduce the externality and it won't result in more-secure software.

Computer security isn't a technological problem—it's an economic problem. Socialists might imagine that companies will improve software security out of the goodness of their hearts, but capitalists know that it needs to be in companies' economic best interest. We'll have fewer vulnerabilities when the entities that have the capability to reduce those vulnerabilities have the economic incentive to do so. And this is why solutions like liability and regulation work.

> "[Software-vendor liability] would only place innovation in peril, surrender U.S. competitive advantage, and risk benefits to customers."

# Software Companies Should Not Be Liable for Internet Security Breaches

*Harris Miller*

*In the following viewpoint, Harris Miller claims that holding software manufacturers liable for security breaches will not improve software security. In fact, he argues, the costs of frivolous lawsuits will reduce innovation and the competitive advantage U.S. software manufacturers have in the global marketplace. Moreover, Miller maintains, software-manufacturer liability shifts responsibility from those who should be held accountable— the cyber criminals themselves. Software quality should be left to the marketplace, he reasons, not to the regulators. Miller is president of the Information Technology Association of America.*

As you read, consider the following questions:

1. According to Miller, how is software like other products of engineering?

2. In the author's opinion, how will lawsuits specifically jeopardize the U.S. software industry's position in global markets?

3. What does the author claim is the technical equivalent of lawsuits aimed at software vendors?

Software-vendor liability continues to be a hot topic as the fallout from several recent intrusions, such as the MS "Blaster" and "SoBig" worms, make headlines. However, heavy-handed regulation imposing sanctions on vendors whose software is breached is the wrong answer.

Such a move [software-vendor liability] would only place innovation in peril, surrender U.S. competitive advantage and risk benefits to customers. Worst of all, perpetrators would face no punishment.

## The Costs of Frivolous Lawsuits

The costs of highly subjective, frivolous lawsuits—the inevitable outcome of new liability laws—would be dramatic. Civil-liability actions against technology makers would:

- *Oversimplify the issue.* Software is not and never can be infallible. It is a product of engineering and expression. Like other products of engineering—automobiles, airplanes, bridges, buildings—the results are not always perfect.

- *Derail innovation.* Market forces are at work so that software companies, service providers, and technology users compete on the basis of security and functionality. The best producers of high-quality, secure software earn the most customers and succeed in this competi-

## The Cost of Liability

Some experts point out that opening software companies to liability would increase the prices charged to consumers and keep them from enjoying the benefits of software features that [companies such as] Microsoft, under threat of litigation, might deem too risky to release. They also say lawsuits wouldn't stop or stem the flow of viruses and worms.

"No matter how careful a software code writer and a manufacturer might be, there is likely to be a more crafty criminal element out there," said lawyer Christopher Wolf, partner in the Washington, D.C., office of law firm Proskauer Rose. "There is no such thing as an absolutely secure piece of software."

*Todd Bishop, "Should Microsoft Be Liable for Bugs?"*
*Seattle Post-Intelligencer, September 12, 2003.*

tive environment. Imposing artificial risk will curb, or even halt, the development of newer and more secure products.

- *Impair U.S. leadership.* Civil-liability lawsuits will harm the U.S. competitive advantage in the $200 billion global software industry. The U.S. plaintiff's bar is unparalleled, and actions by the bar that hinder product development resulting in lost technical jobs and productivity would jeopardize our industry's leading position in global markets.

- *Punish the wrong people.* Pursuing liability for software vulnerabilities shifts the focus away from the wrongdoers. As a country, we need to do a better job of supporting enhanced prosecution of computer crimes.

The marketplace, not legislation, sets expectations for quality, productivity and innovation. Computer use will continue to increase, as will computer crime; the recent worms are proof.

Lawsuits aimed at software vendors for creating products vulnerable to attack are the technical equivalent of charging safe makers with negligence because bank robbers crack safes.

> "It is now time for colleges and universities to take aggressive steps—even when unpopular with students—to combat the piracy of copyrighted material."

# Colleges Should Play a Greater Role in Combating Internet Piracy

**Graham Spanier**

*According to Graham Spanier in the following viewpoint, one mission of colleges and universities is to teach students to respect intellectual property. Unfortunately, he argues, college campuses are often the source of Internet piracy—the online theft of copyrighted work. Colleges and universities should not tolerate copyright infringement on campus, Spanier asserts. Instead, he maintains, they should take aggressive steps such as revoking the Internet access of offending students to combat Internet piracy. Spanier is president of Penn State University.*

As you read, consider the following questions:

1. What does Spanier claim are some of the educational advances information technology provides?

Graham Spanier, "Piracy on the Seas of Higher Education," *Campus Technology*, April 26, 2005. Reproduced by permission.

2. What examples does the author provide to support his assertion that colleges do not teach students to be thieves?

3. What does the author contend is underscored by the filing of lawsuits by the Motion Picture Association of America?

Advances in information technology have allowed universities to gain educational tools we never dreamed of twenty years ago. Engineering classes can meet online to solve problems. Political science students are able to post their papers on class Web sites for peer review. And oceanography researchers are holding video conferences with teams of collaborators from thousands of miles away. But as high-speed Internet access has enabled so many great opportunities at universities across the country, we are faced more than ever with the challenge of using that technology responsibly.

At the core of our mission at Penn State is the creation and dissemination of knowledge. The knowledge created and taught by our faculty is a form of intellectual property. And part of our mission is to support integrity and ethical behavior in respecting such property. But we are now confronted with a tough reality: College campuses have become ground zero for the online piracy of some of our nation's most sought after intellectual property—movies, music, and software.

## A Moral Blind Spot

When we stand by idly and allow our students to abuse the privilege of high-speed Internet access for illegal downloading, we are failing our principles and we are failing our students.

We are not campuses of thieves. Students don't go to the local Blockbuster and walk out with the latest DVD without paying. Undergrads don't go to the campus bookstore and sneak out with a new textbook. So why, we must ask ourselves, do we have such a moral blind spot when it comes to stealing on the Internet?

Our community is grounded in the notion that one's original work—from the poetry of our professors to the discoveries of our scientists—will be recognized and protected. We do a great disservice to our own scholars and creators when we tolerate an environment of copyright infringement.

Sadly, there are tangible consequences to illegal file-sharing beyond compromising our values. The massive quantity of pirated files being uploaded and downloaded in dorm rooms across university campuses is devouring our bandwidth, slowing down our networks, and contributing to the spread of viruses that can wreak havoc on our networks, punishing not just those who illegally share files but everyone else connected to the network.

## Combating Piracy

It is now time for colleges and universities to take aggressive steps—even when unpopular with students—to combat the piracy of copyrighted material that is rampant across the country.

Many of us in the academic community have developed policies for responsible student computer use on campus. At Penn State we have deployed an array of solutions to minimize the trafficking in illegal content, including the provision of free unlimited access to music through an online service paid for by the university. At the same time, those violating our computer policies risk having their access to the network revoked. Other sanctions may be imposed by our Office of Judicial Affairs.

It should not surprise us that the Motion Picture Association of America recently announced that it will begin filing suits against those who steal movies online. This action underscores to a new generation that stealing is stealing, no matter what the method, and that it is wrong and has consequences.

## Sending the Wrong Message

[The members of the Recording Industry Association of America] believe in academic freedom. But academic freedom is not the freedom to steal. Allowing illegal file-sharing is antithetical to any educational institution's objective to instill in its students moral and legal clarity. Colleges and universities are in the education business, preparing young adults to succeed in the world. No administration would teach its students that stealing is okay. But when a school falls to act, it is teaching. Looking the other way when students engage in illegal activity on its system sends a message—and it's the wrong one.

*Cary Sherman, "Combating Internet Piracy on College Campuses,"*
FDCH Congressional Testimony, *September 26, 2006.*

The motion picture and music industries should not have to act alone in trying to hold at bay those who would take their products without permission. As educators and administrators, we should lead by example rather than wait for a wave of lawsuits to force us to change our behavior.

I urge college and university presidents to take up this challenge and promote a change in the culture of campus networking. Stealing is not among our values.

> "Higher education should not be used as the private police force of large corporations."

# Combating Internet Piracy Is Not an Appropriate Role for Colleges

*Mark Luker and Michael Petricone*

*In the following viewpoint, Mark Luker and Michael Petricone argue that colleges should not divert money that should be spent on education to combat Internet piracy. In fact, the authors claim, such efforts will do little to curtail file-sharing. Colleges and universities have already developed educational programs and technologies that support the rights of copyright owners and encourage the fair use of legally acquired content, Luker and Petricone maintain. The authors reason that the fair, noncommercial use of creative content spurs innovation while restriction stifles it. Luker is vice president of EDUCAUSE, and Petricone is senior vice president of the Consumer Electronics Association.*

Mark Luker and Michael Petricone, "Respect for Copyright Comes from Education," *Politico*, December 10, 2007. TM & POLITICO & POLITICO.COM, a division of Allbritton Communications. Reproduced by permission.

As you read, consider the following questions:

1. In the opinion of Luker and Petricone, what did the successful legal battle against file-sharing Web sites such as Grokster show?
2. According to the authors, why is the focus on campus networks misplaced?
3. What do the authors claim is the best way to ensure college students remain good customers?

In his Dec. 4 [2007] opinion piece, "Compiling a Sensible Syllabus for Piracy U," Dan Glickman of the MPAA [Motion Picture Association of America] makes a forceful presentation about the financial harm commercial piracy inflicts on the Hollywood studios and calls for legislation imposing restrictions on campus networks to combat piracy. But there are more effective ways to address the actual sources of the problem without risking even greater harm to the intellectual backbone of our nation, our colleges and universities.

## A Poor Plan

Commercial piracy is wrong, and college students receive this message forcefully from the first day they arrive on campus, along with warnings of fines, network disconnection and other punishment. But, as noted recently by Disney CEO Bob Iger, "The best way to combat piracy is to bring content to market on a well-timed, well-priced basis." As the successful legal battle against file-sharing Web sites like Grokster has shown, simply prevailing in court does little to curtail demand for file-sharing. There is no reason to believe that requiring colleges to implement copyright-owner-developed technologies would fare any better.

Most colleges and universities have already investigated licensing commercial music and movie services, and EDU-CAUSE [whose mission is to advance higher education by promoting the intelligent use of information technology] esti-

## A Chilling Effect on the Marketplace of Ideas

It is critical that higher education institutions set policies that foster open-mindedness and critical inquiry. As Chief Justice Earl Warren noted in *Sweezy v. New Hampshire,* "Teachers and students must always remain free to inquire, to study and to evaluate, to gain new maturity and understanding; otherwise our civilization will stagnate and die."

Monitoring the content of communications is fundamentally incompatible with the mission of educational institutions to foster critical thinking and exploration. Monitoring chills behavior and can squelch creativity that must thrive in educational settings.

*Electronic Privacy Information Center,*
*"EPIC Letter on P2P Monitoring to Colleges and Universities,"*
*November 6, 2002.*

mates that universal adoption could divert as much as $400 million annually from higher education to large corporations. And even on the campuses that have voluntarily deployed these services, they are often rejected by students, even when offered at no charge. The content is often not portable, does not operate on the most popular devices and excludes the musicians many students want.

Glickman's proposal would also require campuses to plan deployment of technological barriers to network file-sharing. But today's technologies are expensive ($200,000 a year or more for a large campus), do not solve the underlying problem, and fail to meet the basic requirements established by campus technology experts.

The focus on campus networks is simply misplaced. Eighty percent of college students live off campus. And of the thousands of infringement lawsuits filed by the RIAA [Recording Industry Association of America] less than 5 percent target college students. Hand-to-hand "social sharing" of physical CDs among friends accounts for far more "piracy" than the Internet.

And yet colleges and universities do take this problem seriously and are continually looking for effective educational approaches. For example, the Digital Freedom Campaign, of which both EDUCAUSE and CEA [Consumer Electronics Association] are members (and to which CEA provides financial support), recently launched Digital Freedom University [DFU] an on-campus educational campaign that helps students understand how to respect copyright while making full use of the benefits of digital content. DFU has also formed an Academic Advisory Board, which includes leading scholars and teachers in digital media and intellectual property. The board is helping to develop educational tools that campus administrations, faculty and students can use to understand and make full use of digital content.

## Spurring Innovation and Creativity

The Digital Freedom Campaign also supports the Freedom and Innovation Revitalizing U.S. Entrepreneurship Act of 2007. This legislation, if enacted, would promote the development of new technologies and enable those who have legally obtained access to digital content to exercise their fair use rights. Copyright is a two-sided coin—there are restrictions that protect copyright owners, but there are also fair use rights that protect the robust noncommercial use of legally acquired content, which spurs innovation and creativity.

An educational effort that focuses only on restriction denies future artists and innovators the opportunity to utilize the constitutionally protected rights of creators. Perversely, this threatens the robust creative activities of future recording artists and movie producers. College students are some of the best customers of digital media and devices, and showing them how to use such products lawfully is the best way to ensure they remain good customers for life.

We join our friends in the content community in encouraging adherence to copyright law, but we disagree with diverting scarce resources from core educational functions to support an industry campaign whose hallmark is suing students. As the Oregon attorney general challenges the RIAA's litigation tactics against university students and even campus administrators, we are reminded that higher education should not be used as the private police force of large corporation. Instead, we should all recognize that the core educational mission of our nation's institutions of higher learning is in many ways directed at the concerns raised by copyright owners.

# Periodical Bibliography

*The following articles have been selected to supplement the diverse views presented in this chapter.*

Grayson Barber — "Greater Data Security, and Cures for Abuse, Are Way Overdue," *New Jersey Law Journal*, December 31, 2007.

Mary Brandel — "Five Ways to Defeat Blog Trolls and Cyberstalkers," *Computer World*, April 27, 2007.

*Chronicle of Higher Education* — "We Must Educate Young People About Cybercrime Before They Start College," January 5, 2007.

*Consumer Reports* — "Costly Credit-Monitoring Services Offer Limited Fraud Protection," April 2007.

*Consumer Reports* — "Laws Have a Chilling Effect on Identity Theft," August 2007.

K. Matthew Dames — "Copyright Clashes on Campus," *Information Today*, May 2007.

William W. Fisher — "Combating Internet Piracy on College Campuses," Statement before the Committee on House Education and the Workforce, Subcommittee on 21st Century Competitiveness, *FDCH Congressional Testimony*, September 26, 2006.

William E. Kirwan — "Combating Internet Piracy on College Campuses," Statement before the Committee on House Education and the Workforce, Subcommittee on 21st Century Competitiveness, *FDCH Congressional Testimony*, September 26, 2006.

Brock Read — "Entertainment Officials Say Colleges Do Too Little to Fight Online Piracy," *Chronicle of Higher Education*, October 13, 2006.

Bruce Schneier — "Paying the Cost of Insecure Software," *Outlook Business*, October 5, 2007.

OPPOSING
VIEWPOINTS®
SERIES

# CHAPTER 4

# What Laws Will Best Prevent Cyber Crime?

# Chapter Preface

In October 2006, after receiving cruel messages on the social-networking site MySpace, thirteen-year old Megan Meier hung herself. She believed that these messages, including one suggesting that the world would be better off without her, came from a sixteen-year-old boy that she had met on the site. In fact, these messages and the boy were a hoax. While the case is extreme and the results rare, it highlights what some commentators claim is an epidemic of cyber-bullying—the use of the Internet or other digital technologies to harass, intimidate, threaten, or defame. "Those who bully and harass stand in the way of learning and threaten the safety of our children," maintains Matt Blunt, governor of Missouri, Megan Meier's home state. Some like-minded analysts believe that new laws are necessary to make cyber-bullying a crime. Others contend, however, that legislators are overreacting and that such laws may violate civil liberties.

Legislators across America are recommending new laws or adding provisions to existing laws to stem what they believe is a growing cyber-bullying problem. In Florida, for example, the state senate, in early 2008, proposed a bill that would require all school districts to develop cyber-bullying polices that allow the districts to punish students who use electronic devices to bully or harass their peers, even if the acts take place off campus or during non-school hours. "By making it law rather than school board policy," reasons Florida State Representative Gary Aubuchon, "we are adding an extra layer of emphasis on how important it is to protect our children at all times."

Opponents of such laws and policies argue that while cyber-bullying is a serious problem with sometimes horrific consequences, new laws are not the solution. "I don't know if it's something that we can legislate away," maintains criminal justice professor Justin W. Patchin. Cases such as the suicide of Megan Meier are tragic, but rare, explains Danah Boyd, who studies teen behavior on MySpace, Facebook, and other social-networking sites at the Berkman Center for Internet and Society at Harvard Law School. "These [new] laws aren't doing anything. What we desperately need is education and discussion," she reasons. Parents and other adults should pay more attention to the pressures and expectations that weigh on today's teens, these observers assert. Some legal analysts such as Thomas Hutton, attorney for the National School Boards Association, worry that a flurry of state cyber-bullying laws will create confusion among school districts as to their scope and power, exposing those who act broadly to liability. More state laws are unnecessary, claims attorney Parry Aftab, because states already have cyber stalking and harassment laws on the books. What is needed, she says, is uniformity "so we know that what's illegal in one state is illegal in the next."

Whether new laws are necessary to protect vulnerable teens like Megan Meier from vicious cyber-bullies remains a controversial question. The authors in the following chapter examine other strategies that they believe will prevent cyber crime.

> "A strong national breach disclosure law is needed in the United States to provide uniform requirements to all organizations as well as mandating meaningful public disclosure."

# A Federal Data Breach Notification Standard Is Necessary

## William Yurcik and Ragib Hasan

*In the following viewpoint, William Yurcik and Ragib Hasan claim that a uniform federal data breach disclosure law will improve the protection of private information such as Social Security, credit card, and bank account numbers. While state laws have helped organizations become accountable for personal data breaches, the laws vary considerably, making it difficult for organizations that do business nationwide to comply, Yurcik and Hasan maintain. A federal law that makes these requirements uniform will make disclosure more meaningful. Yurcik is a senior system engineer and Hasan is a graduate student at the University of Illinois at Urbana-Champaign.*

William Yurcik and Ragib Hasan, "Toward One Strong National Breach Disclosure Law—Justification and Requirements," Workshop on the Economics of Securing the Information Infrastructure, October 23-24, 2006. Reproduced by permission of the authors.

As you read, consider the following questions:

1. According to Yurcik and Hasan, why must networked organization comply separately with each state law?
2. In the authors' opinion, how does monitoring vary from state to state?
3. How do the concerns of privacy and corporate advocates vary, in the authors' view?

State laws in the United States have been very helpful in illuminating breaches of private information by requiring private disclosure between the organization with the breach and the individual owners of the private information that was breached. Although there are currently no public disclosure requirements, these breaches have often been subsequently reported in the mass media.

However, as more states are adopting breach disclosure laws, problems and loopholes are arising that beg a uniform federal law. For instance, state breach disclosure laws do not have uniform requirements, so networked organizations must comply separately with each law—Internet businesses must comply with all state breach disclosure laws. Also state disclosure laws have different triggers and timing that allow organizations to delay, or even forgo, notification of the same breach in different states.

Our position is that a strong national breach disclosure law is needed in the United States to provide uniform requirements to all organizations as well as mandating meaningful public disclosure of all breaches. Such a federal law would eliminate compliance problems between different state laws and provide a valuable tracking mechanism for continually improving the protection of private information.

## The Impact of State Laws

Typical state breach disclosure laws require direct notification between the third party organization with the compromise and each affected individual—without involvement from federal/ state regulator or any level of law enforcement. Private information is defined to be any of the following: Social Security numbers, driver's license number, bank account numbers, credit/debit card numbers, as well as any other personal identifying information.

State disclosure laws are a significant improvement because affected parties would be unaware of their increased risk of identity theft and the public would not know of the size of the problem through mass media reports. However, there are problems. Organizations must assess which state disclosure laws apply to them, a nontrivial task since whether subject to a state law may depend on the location of an organization and/or the residency of those individuals affected. Although state disclosure laws can be categorized into similar groups, each law may have different requirements for notice trigger, timing, content, and recipients.

For an example of the complexity of the problem, some state breach laws require monitoring (per industry best practices) so an organization is vigilant to privacy breaches when they occur. Other state laws require no monitoring. In the states that require monitoring, the type of monitoring is broadly defined, giving organizations wide discretion. Rigorous monitoring may detect more breaches and compel more disclosures under state laws. A low level of monitoring, significantly below industry best practices, may risk customer/ shareholder lawsuits and/or fines from state or federal regulatory agencies (state attorney general, Federal Trade Commission, etc.).

California was the first state with a breach disclosure law in 2003. Since then, thirty-three states have enacted such laws. Since 2005, these laws have resulted in notification of 200+ privacy breaches that would otherwise have been unknown. . . . Breaches are clustered in urban areas where most organizations are based (although no relation to where and how the

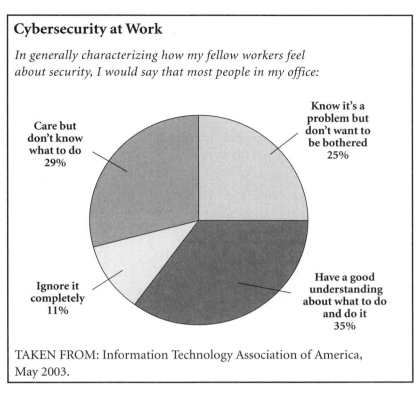

**Cybersecurity at Work**

*In generally characterizing how my fellow workers feel about security, I would say that most people in my office:*

Care but don't know what to do 29%

Know it's a problem but don't want to be bothered 25%

Ignore it completely 11%

Have a good understanding about what to do and do it 35%

TAKEN FROM: Information Technology Association of America, May 2003.

breach occurred). . . . Some states with no disclosure laws which have reported breaches—this is the case where an organization based in a state with no breach disclosure law has a breach event affecting customers based in a state with a breach disclosure law (e.g. California), thus required to disclose per California law although not required to disclose in their own state. This is a frequent occurrence that will likely result in jurisdiction litigation and another example of the need for a uniform national law. . . .

## Toward a National Law

There has been much activity toward a national law with many variations on a theme. Some legislation on simplifying notification procedures which vary widely per states, other legislation seeks to preempt state breach laws altogether with new requirements. Privacy advocates are concerned about a national law with less stringent requirements preempting strong state laws. Corporate advocates are concerned about the costs of notification versus benefits and desensitization due to numerous notifications.

Federal laws already exist with information security requirements specific to particular industries; specifically Gramm-Leach-Bliley (GLB) (financial) and HIPAA [Health Insurance Portability and Accountability Act] (health care). These federal laws require periodic reporting directly to federal regulators with sanctions for non-compliance. However, current federal laws do not have explicit breach disclosure requirements although organizational security status is part of many reports to federal regulations. It is our experience that organizations subject to GLB and HIPAA are careful to hide breach information in security status reports since it is not explicitly required.

## A Strong National Disclosure Law

A national disclosure law is needed for uniform requirements in the following areas:

*Trigger Event:* Some states require the organization with the breach to themselves determine if the compromised private information is "likely" to result in identity theft. Not surprisingly, this has resulted in some organizations not reporting breaches which most objective observers would consider likely to result in identity theft. Other states have a trigger depending on the number of people affected (for instance greater than 1,000 people). Other states exempt certain organizations from having to report. A national law should require all organizations to report all private information breach events.

*Timing:* States require notification following a trigger event over varying periods of time. A standard time should be set that is long enough for an organization to clearly determine the mechanism and extent of the compromise and also short enough so affected individuals can be warned in enough time to protect themselves from increased identity theft risk. We propose a notification timing of ten days from the trigger event (based on our experience in security operations).

*Monitoring and Enforcement:* Some states require organization to monitor their systems to be able to better determine breach events but, as stated previously, the type of monitoring required is vague and changes dynamically. A national breach disclosure law should eliminate the requirement for monitoring but have a significant civil/criminal penalty if a breach is exposed that was not first reported by the organization.

*Type of Notification:* Notification should be written using two-day delivery (not electronic nor telephone).

*Notification Information:* The following information needs to be reported for all breach events to both the affected individuals *and a public clearinghouse* (at present only part of this information is required in many states): (1) number of records breached, (2) type of private information compromised, (3) breach mechanism, (4) number of people affected, (5) estimated cost of breach damage, (6) steps taken to prevent breach from reoccurring, and (7) steps for the affected individual to protect themselves from increased identity theft risk specific to this event.

> *"The federal [notification] bill has be-*
> *come so watered down that it won't be*
> *very effective."*

# Weak Federal Disclosure Laws Will Not Protect Consumers

*Bruce Schneier*

*In the following viewpoint, Bruce Schneier argues that, although a uniform federal data breach disclosure law is a good idea, the laws so far proposed are weak and ineffective. The definition of what constitutes a breach of security is so narrow that notification would not be required in situations that put the personal information of many Americans at risk, he maintains. Moreover, Schneier claims, federal law would preempt much stronger state laws that better protect consumers. Schneier is CTO of Counterpane Internet Security and the author of* Beyond Fear: Thinking Sensible About Security in an Uncertain World.

As you read, consider the following questions:

1. In Schneier's view, why are disclosure laws a good idea?
2. What does the author say happened when security breaches were no longer news?

Bruce Schneier, "The Anti-ID-Theft Bill That Isn't," *Wired News*, April 20, 2006. Reproduced by permission.

3. What, in the author's opinion, is the best way to mitigate the risk of fraud due to impersonation?

California was the first state to pass a law requiring companies that keep personal data to disclose when that data is lost or stolen. Since then, many states have followed suit. Now Congress is debating federal legislation that would do the same thing nationwide.

Except that it won't do the same thing: The federal bill has become so watered down that it won't be very effective. I would still be in favor of it—a poor federal law is better than none—if it didn't also preempt more effective state laws, which makes it a net loss.

Identity theft is the fastest growing area of crime. It's badly named—your identity is the one thing that cannot be stolen—and is better thought of as fraud by impersonation. A criminal collects enough personal information about you to be able to impersonate you to banks, credit card companies, brokerage houses, etc. Posing as you, he steals your money, or takes a destructive joyride on your good credit.

Many companies keep large databases of personal data that is useful to these fraudsters. But because the companies don't shoulder the cost of the fraud, they're not economically motivated to secure those databases very well. In fact, if your personal data is stolen from their databases, they would much rather not even tell you: Why deal with the bad publicity?

## A Good Idea

Disclosure laws force companies to make these security breaches public. This is a good idea for three reasons. One, it is good security practice to notify potential identity theft victims that their personal information has been lost or stolen. Two, statistics on actual data thefts are valuable for research purposes. And three, the potential cost of the notification and the associated bad publicity naturally leads companies to

## Headed in the Right Direction

Disclosure laws do a lot of good things. They provide safeguards for consumers. They also create obligations for companies that are sometimes in denial and don't believe their business can be victimized. . . . Proposed legislation is headed in the right direction, but may water down established state laws because so many entities—business lobbyists and political—will have a hand in creating it.

*A. Bryan Sartin,*
*"Data Breach Notification Makes Sense—Most of the Time,"*
*May 1, 2007. www.CSOonline.com.*

spend more money on protecting personal information—or to refrain from collecting it in the first place.

Think of it as public shaming. Companies will spend money to avoid the PR [Public Relations] costs of this shaming, and security will improve. In economic terms, the law reduces the externalities and forces companies to deal with the true costs of these data breaches.

This public shaming needs the cooperation of the press and, unfortunately, there's an attenuation effect going on. The first major breach after California passed its disclosure law—SB1386—was in February 2005, when ChoicePoint sold personal data on 145,000 people to criminals. The event was all over the news, and ChoicePoint was shamed into improving its security.

Then LexisNexis exposed personal data on 300,000 individuals. And Citigroup lost data on 3.9 million individuals. SB1386 worked; I believe the only reason we knew about these security breaches was because of the law. But the breaches came in increasing numbers, and in larger quantities. After a while, it was no longer news. And when the press stopped reporting, the "cost" of these breaches to the companies declined.

## Lobbyists Weaken Good Law

Today, the only real cost that remains is the cost of notifying customers and issuing cards. It costs banks about $10 to issue a new card, and that's money they would much rather not have to spend. This is the agenda they brought to the federal bill, cleverly titled the Data Accountability and Trust Act or DATA. Lobbyists attacked the legislation in two ways. First, they went after the definition of personal information. Only the exposure of very specific information requires disclosure. For example, the theft of a database that contained people's first initial, middle name, last name, Social Security number, bank account number, address, phone number, date of birth, mother's maiden name and password would not have to be disclosed, because "personal information" is defined as "an individual's first and last name in combination with . . ." certain other personal data.

Second, lobbyists went after the definition of "breach of security." The latest version of the bill reads: "The term 'breach of security' means the unauthorized acquisition of data in electronic form containing personal information that establishes a reasonable basis to conclude that there is a significant risk of identity theft to the individuals to whom the personal information relates."

Get that? If a company loses a backup tape containing millions of individuals' personal information, it doesn't have to disclose if it believes there is no "significant risk of identity theft." If it leaves a database exposed, and has absolutely no audit logs of who accessed that database, it could claim it has no "reasonable basis" to conclude there is a significant risk. Actually, the company could probably point to a study that showed the probability of fraud to someone who has been the victim of this kind of data loss to be less than 1 in 1,000—which is not a "significant risk"—and then not disclose the data breach at all.

Even worse, this federal law preempts the twenty-three existing state laws—and others being considered—many of which contain stronger individual protections. So while DATA might look like a law protecting consumers nationwide, it is actually a law protecting companies with large databases *from* state laws protecting consumers.

So in its current form, this legislation would make things worse, not better.

## An Uncertain Future

Of course, things are in flux. They're *always* in flux. The language of the bill has changed regularly [in 2006] as various committees got their hands on it. There's also another bill, HR3997, which is even worse. And even if something passes, it has to be reconciled with whatever the Senate passes, and then voted on again. So no one really knows what the final language will look like.

But the devil is in the details, and the only way to protect us from lobbyists tinkering with the details is to ensure that the federal bill does not preempt any state bills: that the federal law is a minimum, but that states can require more.

That said, disclosure is important, but it's not going to solve identity theft. As I've written previously, the reason theft of personal information is so common is that the data is so valuable. The way to mitigate the risk of fraud due to impersonation is not to make personal information harder to steal, it's to make it harder to use.

Disclosure laws only deal with the economic externality of data brokers protecting your personal information. What we really need are laws prohibiting credit card companies and other financial institutions from granting credit to someone using your name with only a minimum of authentication.

But until that happens, we can at least hope that Congress will refrain from passing bad bills that override good state laws—and helping criminals in the process.

> *"The Convention on Cybercrime minimizes the barriers to international cooperation that currently impede investigations and prosecutions on computer-related crimes."*

# The Cybercrime Treaty Will Improve the Global Fight Against Internet Crime

## Cyber Security Industry Alliance

*In the following viewpoint, the Cyber Security Industry Alliance (CSIA) claims that cyber crime poses a serious international threat. CSIA argues that cyber criminals sometimes operate in a different nation from their victims and laws vary between nations, so pursing and prosecuting cyber criminals can be challenging. The Convention on Cybercrime removes legal barriers and promotes international cooperation in cyber crime investigation and prosecution, CSIA maintains. Moreover, CSIA asserts, the convention does not require cooperation in cases that would violate U.S. civil liberties. CSIA is a coalition of information security providers who shape cyber security policies.*

As you read, consider the following questions:

1. According to CSIA, what does the Cybercrime Convention do to ensure that law enforcement officials have the authority to investigate and prosecute?
2. How many countries have ratified the convention as of July 2007?
3. In CSIA's opinion, will any new legislation be required by the United States after ratification of the convention?

The Council of Europe's Convention on Cybercrime is the first and only international, multilateral treaty specifically addressing the need for cooperation in the investigation and prosecution of computer network crimes. It promotes global law enforcement cooperation with respect to searches and seizures and provides timely extradition for computer network-based crimes covered under the treaty.

The Council of Europe is a negotiating forum established in 1949 to uphold and strengthen human rights, and promote democracy and the rule of law in Europe. Its forty-four sovereign state members include all the European Union. For years, the United States has participated in many Council-sponsored conventions related to criminal matters.

## The Status and Scope of the Convention

The Cybercrime Convention requires parties to establish laws against cybercrime to ensure that their law enforcement officials have the necessary procedural authority to investigate and prosecute computer-related offenses, and to provide international cooperation to other parties in the fight against cybercrime. Like other multi-lateral conventions, the framework is flexible to allow for adaptation by a variety of legal systems.

The Cybercrime Convention entered into force on July 1, 2004. As of July 2007, the Convention has been signed by thirty-nine Member States of the Council of Europe and four Non-Member States. Twenty-one countries have ratified the Convention and entered it into force, including the U.S. . . .

## Why Is the Cybercrime Convention Important?

Cybercrime poses a huge threat to global society. One reason is the profound, fundamental change by technology in the way people live, work and communicate. Cybercrime is more far-reaching than traditional crime because it transcends geographical and national boundaries. In recent years, fast-moving computer viruses and worms have temporarily disrupted business operations and emergency services worldwide.

Cybercrime is also challenging existing legal concepts, particularly since it transcends sovereign borders. Cyber-criminals are often in places other than where their crime hits victims. The Council of Europe engineered the Cybercrime Convention to resolve these legal issues and promote a common, co-operative approach to prosecuting people who commit cyber-crime.

The Convention on Cybercrime minimizes the barriers to international cooperation that currently impede investigations and prosecutions of computer-related crimes, making it an important tool in the global fight against those who seek to disrupt computer networks, misuse sensitive or private information, or commit traditional crimes using Internet-enabled technologies.

## The U.S. Contribution

The idea for the Convention on Cybercrime grew from studies by the Council of Europe in 1989 and 1995. The Council established a committee to draft the Convention, which was finished in May 2001, and opened for signing and ratification on November 23, 2001.

The United States was invited as an "observer" to the two studies and helped develop the final Convention, which in-

## What Benefits is the Convention on Cybercrime Expected to Bring for the United States?

The United States has much to gain from a strong, well-crafted multilateral instrument that removes or minimizes the many procedural and jurisdictional obstacles that can delay or endanger international investigations and prosecutions of computer-related crimes.

The Convention breaks new ground by being the first multilateral agreement drafted specifically to address the problems posed by the international nature of computer crime. Although we believe that the obligations and powers that the Convention requires the United States to undertake are already provided for under U.S. law, the Convention makes progress in this area by (1) requiring signatory countries to establish certain substantive offenses in the area of computer crime, (2) requiring parties to adopt domestic procedural laws to investigate computer crimes, and (3) providing a solid basis for international law enforcement cooperation in combating crime committed through computer systems.

*U.S. Department of Justice,*
*Council of Europe Convention on Cybercrime, FAQs and Answers,*
*November 10, 2003.*

cluded several drafts made available for public comment. Active U.S. participants in the development process included representatives from the Departments of Justice, State and Commerce who closely worked with other U.S. government agencies and interested private parties. U.S. government representatives also met with members of the U.S. technology and communications industry plus public interest groups during

2000 and 2001 to gather and incorporate comments on draft provisions of the Convention. Based on this feedback, the United States sought and obtained important revisions to the Convention and its Explanatory Report.

There is no new legislation required by the United States after its ratification of the Convention on Cybercrime. The Convention allows reservations and declarations by signatories for exemption from particular provisions that contradict national law. The United States had a number of reservations and declarations attached to its ratification that protect the Constitutional rights of American citizens.

## The Role of the European Union and Its Member States

The European Commission participated as an observer in the negotiations on the Cybercrime Convention. The Convention was signed by all EU [European Union] Member States; however, not all of them have ratified it. For example, ratification is still pending in countries like Belgium, Germany, Spain and the United Kingdom. In its recent Communication "Towards a general policy on the fight against cybercrime," adopted in May 2007, the European Commission calls upon EU Member States and relevant third countries to ratify the Convention. In addition, the European Commission commits itself to looking into the possibility for the European Community to become a party to the Convention.

The Convention provides for limitations on assistance to other countries. This enables its parties to deny assistance in a variety of circumstances. For instance, the United States could deny assistance if an investigation would violate its First Amendment guarantees.

CSIA [Cyber Security Industry Alliance] joined other industry organizations as an active supporter of the Cybercrime Convention and was instrumental to achieving U.S. ratification of the Convention in September 2006. CSIA urges other participating countries to consider ratification of the Convention and further expand international cooperation in the fight against cybercrime.

> *"Though it won't prevent crime, the Cybercrime Treaty will make your online privacy subject to the whims of 'law enforcement' officials in foreign nations."*

# The Cybercrime Treaty Threatens Civil Liberties

*Bob Barr*

*According to Bob Barr in the following viewpoint, the Cybercrime Treaty creates an international legal process that threatens the civil liberties of American citizens. For example, the treaty allows law enforcement officials in other nations to gain access to the private information of U.S. citizens even if the laws of that nation would violate U.S. laws, he maintains. Moreover, Barr argues, increasing international law enforcement access to private information will only increase the likelihood of cyber fraud, not decrease it. Barr is a former Republican member of the U.S. House of Representatives from Georgia and a former U.S. Attorney.*

As you read, consider the following questions:

1. Why, in Barr's view, have most Americans not heard about the Cybercrime Treaty?

Bob Barr, "Trashing Privacy," The *Washington Times*, August 20, 2006. Reproduced by permission.

2. What specific examples does the author provide to show the danger posed by the Cybercrime Treaty?

3. How does the author say the damage of passing the treaty can be minimized?

Thanks to the U.S. Senate's remarkable but well-known lack of backbone, nations such as Albania, Croatia, Uganda and many others now will be able to call up the U.S. Justice Department and find out as much as they would like about anything you do with your computer.

At this point, you probably wonder why you haven't read about this. Frankly, there's not much reason you would have, unless you read some relatively obscure publications that focus mostly on technology issues. Another reason you wouldn't likely have heard of it is, of course, that most major media outlets ignored the issue entirely, largely due to how the Senate essentially trashed your online privacy by voice vote the night before heading home for another summer recess.

## The Treaty's Broad Reach

The issue at hand is the so-called Cybercrime Treaty, drafted by European bureaucrats and championed by the Bush administration. The treaty creates an international law enforcement mechanism for investigators in any signatory country to gain access to private information in another country (such as the United States). In essence, these other nations now can "borrow" law enforcement officers of another nation (again, most likely the United States), and use them to investigate any alleged crimes that involved somehow, at some point, using a computer.

For example, a cop in South Africa might be investigating an online poker site that has violated some obscure provisions of South African law. Let's then say you visited that same poker site, played a few hands with a South African national and logged out. Under this new treaty, the South African gov-

## Prosecuting Constitutionally Protected Activities

The American Civil Liberties Union [ACLU] spelled out some of the problems [of the Cybercrime Treaty]. "France and Germany have laws prohibiting the advertisement for sale of Nazi memorabilia or even discussing Nazi philosophy, activities that are protected in the United States under the First Amendment, the letter said. These countries could demand assistance from the United States to investigate and prosecute individuals for activities that are constitutionally protected in this country."

*Declan McCullagh,*
*"Fuzzy Logic Behind Bush's Cybercrime Treaty,"*
ZDNet News, *November 28, 2005.*

ernment can demand that U.S. federal agents visit your Internet Service Provider or ISP, demand from that ISP access about your online activities, and turn that information over to the foreign government. Of course, this would all happen without your knowledge.

Similarly, if law enforcement officials in another signatory nation with much stricter gun control laws than ours, decide there's some evidence on a U.S. citizen's computer in this country that they say is related to an anti-firearms prosecution, all they need do is ring up our Justice Department and request the information. It matters not that the offense in the other country triggering the investigation might not be a crime under U.S. law.

## Ineffective and Invasive

Aside from this treaty's overly broad reach, it will do little or nothing to accomplish its stated purpose: fighting true, computer-related crime. The Internet's reality is that it is completely borderless. A criminal investigated in one country can simply pull up stakes and locate his activities to another country that has not signed the Cybercrime Treaty. A credit card fraud ring can simply operate just as well from Cambodia as it from Canada; all it needs is an active connection to the Internet.

Though it won't prevent crime, the Cybercrime Treaty will make your online privacy subject to the whims of "law enforcement" officials in foreign nations. If you think your personal information is safe in the hands of the governments of places like Albania, Croatia and Uganda, think again. The private information they obtain via this treaty is about as likely to be used to commit fraud as to prevent it.

Most senators who voted to ratify the treaty are blissfully unaware of, or unconcerned about, these facts. The leadership, at the White House's request, decided to vote on the treaty without any substantive hearings or floor debate. It was approved by voice vote, so no senator had to take a public position on it.

Though the treaty has been passed, there may still be some way to minimize the damage it can wreak on citizens' online privacy. The House, for example, could withhold funds from U.S. agencies to spend on enforcing it.

In the final analysis, it is critical that all Americans who care about computer privacy, and all who may be concerned about the long reach of regimes in other countries to invade their privacy, quickly launch a flanking move to derail this latest power grab by a Republican president and Senate. Otherwise, any tinhorn despot in another country will be able to easily find out what you've ordered on the Internet or to whom you've sent your latest politically motivated e-mail.

> *"Legal actions were directed at college and university students around the county. The inclusion of so many students was unprecedented. Unfortunately, it was also necessary."*

# A Crackdown on Student Internet Copyright Infringers Is Necessary

## Mitch Bainwol and Cary Sherman

*In the following viewpoint, Mitch Bainwol and Cary Sherman argue that, although the Recording Industry Association of America (RIAA) has made progress combating Internet piracy, college students continue to download music illegally. As a result, the authors claim, RIAA has been forced to prosecute students who engage in illegal sharing of copyrighted material using peer-to-peer (P2P) networks. Until colleges and universities implement recommended technologies to limit Internet piracy of protected artistic work, RIAA will be forced to rigorously pursue student offenders. Bainwol is chairman and CEO of RIAA, and Sherman is president of RIAA.*

As you read, consider the following questions:

1. In the opinion of Bainwol and Sherman, what has been the impact of the online sharing of copyrighted music, movies, software, and other works?

2. According to college students surveyed by NPD, what percentage of the music they acquired was obtained illegally?

3. Why do the authors believe that Internet piracy is not the problem of organizations such as RIAA alone?

As many in the higher education community are well aware from news coverage ... the Recording Industry Association of America (RIAA), on behalf of its member labels, recently initiated a new process for lawsuits against computer users who engage in illegal file-trafficking of copyrighted content on peer-to-peer (P2P) systems. In the new round of lawsuits, 400 of these legal actions were directed at college and university students around the country. The inclusion of so many students was unprecedented. Unfortunately, it was also necessary.

In the three and a half years since we first began suing individuals for illegal file-trafficking, we have witnessed an immense growth in national awareness of this problem. Today, virtually no one, particularly technology, savvy students, can claim not to know that the online "sharing" of copyrighted music, movies, software and other works is illegal. By now, there is broad understanding of the impact from this activity, including billions of dollars in lost revenue, millions of dollars in lost taxes, thousands of lost jobs, and entire industries struggling to grow viable legitimate online market places that benefit consumers against a backdrop of massive theft.

## A Significant Problem

We have made great progress—both in holding responsible the illicit businesses profiting from copyright infringement and in deterring many individuals from engaging in illegal downloading behavior. Nevertheless, illegal file-trafficking remains a significant and disproportionate problem on college campuses. A recent survey by *Student Monitor*, from spring 2006, found that more than half of college students download music and movies illegally, and according to the market research firm NPD, college students alone accounted for more than 1.3 billion illegal music downloads in 2006.

We know some in the university community believe these figures overstate the contribution of college students to the illegal file-trafficking problem today. Yet new data confirms that students are more prone to engaging in this illegal activity than the population at large. While college students represented only 10 percent of the sample in the online NPD study, they accounted for 26 percent of all music downloading on P2P networks and 21 percent of all P2P users in 2006. Furthermore, college students surveyed by NPD reported that more than two-thirds of all the music they acquired was obtained illegally.

Moreover, our focus on university students is not detracting from our continuing enforcement efforts against individuals using commercial Internet Service Provider (ISP) accounts to engage in this same behavior. Indeed, we have asked ISPs to participate in the same new process that we have implemented for university network users.

## A Teachable Moment

Yet this is about far more than the size of a particular slice of the pie. This is about a generation of music fans. College students used to be the music industry's best customers. Now, finding a record store still in business anywhere near a campus is a difficult assignment at best. It's not just the loss of current sales that concerns us, but the habits formed in college that will stay with these students for a lifetime. This is a teachable moment—an opportunity to educate these particular students about the importance of music in their lives and the importance of respecting and valuing music as intellectual property.

The prevalence of this activity on our college campuses should be as unacceptable to universities as it is to us. These networks are intended for educational and research purposes. These are the environments where students receive the guidance necessary to become responsible citizens. Institutions of higher education, of all places, are where people should learn about the value of intellectual property and the importance of protecting it.

The fact that students continue to engage in this behavior is particularly egregious given the extraordinary lengths to which we have gone to address the problem. Our approach always has been and continues to be collaborative—partnering with and appealing to the higher motives of universities. We have met personally with university administrators. We have provided both instructional material and educational resources, including an orientation video to help deter illegal downloading. We have worked productively through organizations like the Joint Committee of the Higher Education and Entertainment Communities. We have participated in Congressional hearings.

We have informed schools of effective network technologies to inhibit illegal activity. We have licensed legitimate music services at steeply discounted rates for college students and helped to arrange partnership opportunities between universities and legitimate services. We have stepped up our notice program to alert schools and students of infringing activity. And, of course, we have as a last resort brought suit against individual file-traffickers.

## A Last Resort

With this latest round of lawsuits, we have initiated a new pre-lawsuit settlement program intended to allow students to

voluntarily settle claims before a suit is actually filed. We have asked for school administrations' assistance in passing our letters on to students in order to give them the opportunity to settle a claim at a discounted rate and before a public record is created. This is a program initiated in part as a response to defendants who told us they would like this opportunity, and we are encouraged by the swift response of so many schools. Lawsuits are by no means our desired course of action. But when the problem continues to persist, year after year, we are left with no choice.

An op-ed writer recently published in this forum described this approach as bullying. There is a big difference between using "bullying tactics" and using a "bully pulpit" to make an important point. Should we ignore this problem and stand silent as entire generations of students learn to steal? Should we not point out that administrators are brushing off responsibility, choosing not to exercise their moral leadership on this issue? This problem is anything but ours and ours alone. If music is stolen with such impunity, what makes term papers any different? Yet we know university administrators very aggressively pursue plagiarism. Why would universities—so prolific in the creation of intellectual capital themselves—not apply the same high standards to intellectual property of all kinds? This is, after all, a segment of our economy responsible for more than 6 percent of our nation's GDP [gross domestic product].

Furthermore, a Business Software Alliance study conducted last year found that 86 percent of managers say that the file-sharing attitudes and behaviors of applicants affect on their hiring decisions. Don't administrators have an obligation to prepare students for the real world, where theft is simply not tolerated? Our strategy is not to bully but to point out that the self-interest of universities lies remarkably close to the interests of the entertainment industries whose products are being looted. And, most importantly, we have sought to do so in a collaborative way.

It doesn't have to be like this. We take this opportunity to once again ask schools to be proactive, to step up and accept responsibility for the activity of their students on their network—not legal responsibility, but moral responsibility, as educators, as organizations transmitting values. Turning a blind eye will not make the problem go away; it will further ingrain in students the belief that a costly and illegal pastime is sanctioned, and even facilitated, by school administrations.

## How Schools Can Help

The necessary steps are simple. First, implement a network technical solution. Products like Red Lambda's cGrid are promising as effective and comprehensive solutions that maintain the integrity, security, and legal use of school computing systems without threatening student privacy. Some schools have used these products to block the use of P2P entirely, realizing that the overwhelming, if not sole, use of these applications on campus is to illegally download and distribute copyrighted works. For schools that do not wish to prohibit entirely access to P2P applications, products such as Audible Magic's CopySense can be used to filter illegal P2P traffic, again, without impinging on student privacy.

Second, offer a legal online service to give students an inexpensive alternative to stealing. One such service, Ruckus, is funded through advertising and is completely free to users. When schools increasingly provide their students with amenities like cable TV, there is simply no reason not to offer them cheap or free legal access to the music they crave.

Third, take appropriate and consistent disciplinary action when students are found to be engaging in infringing conduct online. This includes stopping and punishing such activity in dorms and on all Local Area Networks throughout a school's computing system.

Some administrations have embraced these solutions, engaged in productive dialogue with us to address this problem, and begun to see positive results. We thank these schools and commend them for their responsible actions.

Yet the vast majority of institutions still have not come to grips with the need to take appropriate action. As we continue our necessary enforcement measures—including our notices and pre-lawsuit settlement initiative—and as Congress continues to monitor this issue with a watchful eye, we hope these schools will fully realize the harm their inaction causes them and their students. We call upon them to do their part to address this continuing, mutual problem.

> "Students are going to copy what they want, when they want, from whom they want."

# A Crackdown on Student File-Sharing Is an Ineffective Strategy

*Fred von Lohmann*

*In the following viewpoint, Fred von Lohmann claims that pressuring universities to install expensive technology and threatening students with federal lawsuits will not prevent illegal file-sharing. Technological efforts to block file-sharing will simply be met with counter technology developed by clever computer science students, he maintains. Moreover, von Lohmann asserts, universities should spend scare funds to prepare students for the genuine problems facing future generations. An attorney with the Electronic Frontier Foundation, von Lohmann represented one of the defendants in* MGM v. Grokster, *a landmark file-sharing case.*

As you read, consider the following questions:

1. In von Lohmann's view, what do Columbia, Vanderbilt, Duke, Howard, and UCLA have in common?

Fred von Lohmann, "Copyright Silliness on Campus," The *Washington Post*, June 6, 2007. Reproduced by permission of the author.

2. What would students completely cut off from the Internet continue to do, in the author's opinion,?

3. What does the author claim universities should do in response to threats and pressure?

What do Columbia, Vanderbilt, Duke, Howard and UCLA have in common? Apparently, leaders in Congress think that they aren't expelling enough students for illegally swapping music and movies.

## A Futile Battle

The House committees responsible for copyright and education wrote a joint letter May 1 scolding the presidents of nineteen major American universities, demanding that each school respond to a six-page questionnaire detailing steps it has taken to curtail illegal music and movie file-sharing on campus. One of the questions—"Does your institution expel violating students?"—shows just how out of control the futile battle against campus downloading has become.

As universities are pressured to punish students and install expensive "filtering" technologies to monitor their computer networks, the entertainment industry has ramped up its student shakedown campaign. The Recording Industry Association of America has targeted more than 1,600 individual students in the past four months, demanding that each pay $3,000 for file-sharing transgressions or face a federal lawsuit. In total, the music and movie industries have brought more than 20,000 federal lawsuits against individual Americans in the past three years.

History is sure to judge harshly everyone responsible for this absurd state of affairs. Our universities have far better things to spend money on than bullying students. Artists deserve to be fairly compensated, but are we really prepared to sue and expel every college student who has made an illegal copy? No one who takes privacy and civil liberties seriously

## The RIAA Campaign Has Failed

The RIAA's [Recording Industry Association of America's] campaign of suing individual American music fans has failed. It has failed to curtail P2P downloading. It has not persuaded music fans that sharing is equivalent to shoplifting. It has not put a penny into the pockets of artists. It has failed to drive the bulk of file-sharers into the arms of authorized music services. In fact, the RIAA lawsuits may well be driving file-sharers to new technologies that will be much harder for the RIAA's investigators to infiltrate and monitor.

*Electronic Frontier Foundation,*
RIAA v. The People: Four Years Later, *August 2002.*

can believe that the installation of surveillance technologies on university computer networks is a sensible solution.

It's not an effective solution, either. Short of appointing a copyright hall monitor for every dorm room, there is no way digital copying will be meaningfully reduced. Technical efforts to block file-sharing will be met with clever countermeasures from sharp computer science majors. Even if students were completely cut off from the Internet, they would continue to copy CDs, swap hard drives and pool their laptops.

Already, a hard drive capable of storing more than 80,000 songs can be had for $100. Blank DVDs, each capable of holding more than a first-generation iPod, now sell for a quarter apiece. Students are going to copy what they want, when they want, from whom they want.

## What Universities Can Do

So universities can't stop file-sharing. But they can still help artists get paid for it. How? By putting some cash on the bar.

Universities already pay blanket fees so that student a cappella groups can perform on campus, and they also pay for cable TV subscriptions and site licenses for software. By the same token, they could collect a reasonable amount from their students for "all you can eat" downloading.

The recording industry is already willing to offer unlimited downloads with subscription plans for $10 to $15 per month through services such as Napster and Rhapsody. But these services have been a failure on campuses, for a number of reasons, including these: They don't work with the iPod; they cause downloaded music to "expire" after students leave the school; and they don't include all the music students want.

The only solution is a blanket license that permits students to get unrestricted music and movies from sources of their choosing.

At its heart, this is a fight about money, not about morality. We should have the universities collect the cash, pay it to the entertainment industry, and let the students do what they are going to do anyway. In exchange, the entertainment industry should call off the lawyers and lobbyists, leaving our nation's universities to focus on the real challenges facing America's next generation of leaders.

> "Cyberpredators can reach across state lines to terrorize their victims wherever they live and work. [Cyberstalking victims] need the protection that only the federal government can provide."

# A Federal Cyber-Stalking Law Will Protect Victims

*Jim McDermott*

*In the following viewpoint, Jim McDermott argues that cyberstalking is a serious problem that threatens many Americans. Although some states have laws to pursue and prosecute those who stalk their victims online, the Internet has no borders and cyberpredators can easily cross state lines to bully their victims, McDermott maintains. Cyber-stalking is a twenty-first century crime that requires a twenty-first century solution—a strong national law that will protect victims and punish cyber-predators, the author asserts. McDermott is a U.S. congressman from the 7th congressional district of Washington state.*

As you read, consider the following questions:

1. According to McDermott, how did Joelle Ligon's cyber-stalker first contact her?

Jim McDermott, "Cyberstalking," Speech Before the House, May 5, 2004.

2. When did law enforcement get a break in Joelle's cyber-stalking case?

3. What does the author claim is the first step to ensure all Americans are safe from cyber-stalkers?

A merica now knows the name of a woman who lives in my congressional district in Seattle. But she did not seek fame and would prefer anonymity.

## A Victim and an Advocate

Her name is Joelle Ligon. I rise to speak about her plight, her courage, and the need for this Congress to act. Joelle deserves to live her life without fear, as everybody deserves. Unfortunately, Joelle's life was turned into a nightmare because of cyberstalking.

Today she is both a victim and an advocate, and she was invited to share her story the other day on "Good Morning America." It was not easy for Joelle, but she knew it was important to warn America about the dangers lurking online. Joelle was fifteen when she met and dated an eighteen-year-old young man in high school. Nothing unusual about that. Eventually Joelle severed the relationship and moved on with her life. She married and began a career. A few years later, Joelle received an e-mail one day. It was supposedly sent from a woman she did not know, but whoever sent it knew her. Then a second e-mail came with more personal details that no stranger could possibly know. Joelle began to suspect that the woman was really a man. By the third e-mail, Joelle was sure the e-mails were coming from her former high school boyfriend. She wrote back, naming him, and telling him to stop. Things went from bad to bizarre. The e-mails got much worse. They began to include pornography and threats like this: "Not only is it bad karma to have enemies, I'm a bad enemy to have."

Joelle was terrified. Then came phone calls in the middle of the night. Her phone number had been posted online by someone urging men to call her for sex. Joelle went to the local police, but they concluded there was nothing they could do because no law had been broken. Joelle and her husband moved to Seattle, but within months the nightmare came back. Joelle started receiving calls at work from men who had seen her number posted online in sex chat rooms. She again went to the local police and to the FBI, but nothing was done. Finally, her co-workers and supervisors received an e-mail that accused her of falsifying her employment credentials and of sexual misconduct. The city of Seattle's computer security officer, Kirk Bailey, became the white knight. He got people involved, but progress was painfully slow because no laws specifically address cyberstalking. Eventually an assistant U.S. Attorney got involved, but finding a law to deal with a twenty-first century crime has been tough.

A break in the case came when the ex used her phone number in a chat room. Authorities acted, using title 47 of the Telecommunications Act for the first time in a case like this. The ex-boyfriend has been charged, but it has taken years and a courageous woman willing to see it through.

## A National Problem

And it is not over yet. Joelle and millions of other Americans need our help. By some estimates, one out of every twelve women in America is stalked online. The problem extends to men as well. Some states, including Washington have acted to toughen the laws, but it is time to recognize that cyberstalking is a national problem. We are using a twentieth century law to fight twenty-first century crime. That has to change. Cyberspace has no state borders. Cyberpredators can reach across state lines to terrorize their victims wherever they live and work. [Cyberstalking victims] need the protection that only the federal government can provide. We need to modernize our laws to make sure they protect Joelle and every American.

## Three Basic Types of Stalkers

- A simple *obsessional stalker* is anything but simple. They are typically the person who refuses to believe that a relationship is over, although they have been told repeatedly that it is. This is the most common type of stalker.

- The next type is the *delusional stalker*, they frequently have never had any contact with their victim beyond the boundaries of their own mind. They may suffer from mental illness like schizophrenia, bipolar disorder or erotomania. What they have in common is a false belief that keeps them tied to their victims. In erotomania, they believe that the victim loves them, even though they have never met. . . .

- The last type of stalker is the *vengeful stalker*. They get angry at their victim due to some slight either real or imagined. We have all heard of disgruntled employees, these are vengeful stalkers and can be just as dangerous as the delusional. They stalk to get even and believe that "they" have been victimized. Ex-spouses can turn into this type of stalker and violence is all too common a result.

*www.wiredsafety.org,*
*Cyber911 Emergency: Cyberstalker profile, (n.d.).*

Cyberspace has opened doors we are just beginning to understand. This one, we already know. Everyone has the right to feel safe and be safe. Anything less is wrong and should be illegal with severe penalties. The first step is awareness. I am preparing a letter to circulate to my colleagues that will include newspaper accounts from Seattle about Joelle. We are going to work with the appropriate members and committees in the House as soon as possible to tackle cyberstalking head-on. We will do what we need to do to clarify and strengthen our laws.

I urge both Republicans and Democrats to join me in protecting Joelle, to join me in protecting every American. Let the predators know that they are the only ones who should not feel safe today.

Joelle, you are not alone. Help is coming.[1]

---

1. On January 5, 2006, President George W. Bush signed into law Section 113 of the Violence Against Women Act, which prohibits anyone from using a telecommunications device "without disclosing his identity and with intent to annoy, abuse, threaten, or harass any person."

*"[The Preventing Cyberstalking law] may seek to protect against real threats or violence but its language is so vague as to endanger much broader political discussion."*

# The Federal Cyber-Stalking Law Violates Free Speech

*Wendy McElroy*

*In the following viewpoint, Wendy McElroy claims that the cyber-stalking law added to the Violence Against Women Act is overly broad and, therefore, threatens free speech. The law prohibits using a telecommunications device such as a computer to "annoy, abuse, threaten, or harass any person," she maintains. However, McElroy argues, while Internet speech such as an anonymous post on a blog that criticizes a politician or a political action might be annoying, it is protected speech. However, under the new law, she reasons, because it is annoying, such speech might be unconstitutionally prohibited. McElroy is a libertarian, feminist writer.*

As you read, consider the following questions:

1. According to McElroy, what are some of the penalties for violation of the telecommunications statute?

2. What are the First Amendment exceptions to stating opinions under a pen name, according the author?

3. What distinction does Section 113 fail to make, in the author's opinion?

Fiery debate surrounds Section 113 of the Violence Against Women Act—a last minute addition to the act titled Preventing Cyberstalking.

Is the new law 'evil' or merely redundant? Will it destroy Internet communications as we know them or have no effect? Do members of Congress actually read the measures upon which they vote?

Section 113 was signed into law by President Bush on January 5 [2006]. It amends 47 U.S.C. 223, the telecommunications harassment statute that is rooted in the Communications Act of 1934.

The telecommunications statute prohibits anyone from using a telephone or a telecommunications device "without disclosing his identity and with intent to annoy, abuse, threaten, or harass any person."

In application this has meant that you cannot anonymously annoy another person through the phone lines. Penalties include two years in prison and onerous fines.

Section 113 amends the statute to include "any device or software that can be used to originate telecommunications or other types of communications that are transmitted, in whole or in part, by the Internet." . . .

## Challenging the Cyberstalking Law

On January 9 [2006], electronic-freedom guru Declan McCullagh published an article entitled "Create an e-annoyance, go to jail." Almost instant furor ensued.

McCullagh opened by declaring, "It's no joke. Last Thursday, President [George W.] Bush signed into law a prohibition on posting annoying Web messages or sending annoying e-mail messages without disclosing your true identity."

McCullagh and those who agree with his interpretation of Section 113 represent 'the law is evil and will damage the Internet' side of the debate. Their warnings revolve around the two "A"s: "annoyance" and "anonymous."

## Constitutional Arguments

First Amendment scholar Eugene Volokh argues that Section 113, if consistently applied, will criminalize annoying Web speech that is also meant to inform. For example, the anonymous creator of a blog that criticizes a politician may sincerely wish the target to become uncomfortable enough with public backlash to change his or her behavior. If the site engages in damaging lies, then existing libel laws apply.

Otherwise, the right to state opinions under a pen name has been generally recognized by the First Amendment, with certain exceptions such as threats.

The parallel of a 'pen name' is significant because Section 113 does not merely extend traditional protections from an old technology (phones) to a new one (the Internet). The Web is more like publishing than telecommunication. Phone calls are considered one-on-one communications and so, as Volokh comments, they are "rarely of very much First Amendment value."

By contrast, the Internet is public speech. This fact alone makes Section 113 different in kind from 47 U.S.C. 223 and not merely an extension of the same principle.

Moreover, "annoyance" and "intent to annoy" are unconstitutionally vague terms. By contrast, harassment seems well defined: stalking, impersonating someone, threats, sending viruses through e-mail, libel, contacting a target's family and co-

## The Impact of Section 113

Taken to a logical extreme conclusion, it is possible that a person who makes a Web posting or who sends an e-mail that is intended simply to "annoy" someone else while not disclosing his or her true identity, could be subject to fines and jail time.

So much for freedom of speech—so much for appropriate Internet anonymity. . . .

While Cyberstalking certainly should be prevented . . . we should be careful not to erode our constitutionality protected rights.

*Eric J. Sinrod,*
*"The Erosion of Anonymous Internet Speech:*
*New Federal Law to Prohibit 'Cyberstalking,'"*
*FindLaw Writ, January 27, 2006.*

workers. Critics of Section 113 are "not" defending a "right" to harass but the right to be publicly annoying, which is no more than freedom of speech.

As someone who runs electronic bulletin boards, I've seen both harassment and annoyance in practice. Annoyance is when a churlish poster uses a screen name to flame another member because of a comment on Iraq or abortion. Harassment is what recently led to my closing a bulletin board; a member's real name was "outed" and his "real life" was shadowed by threats.

As it stands, Section 113 makes no distinction between childish and menacing behavior.

Interestingly, those who argue against McCullagh do not necessarily argue for Section 113. Rather, they point to the irrelevance of the "annoyance" reference. Former Justice Department prosecutor Orin Kerr states that the statute and VAWA

[Violence Against Women Act] amendment can only be used to prohibit speech that is not protected by the First Amendment. In short, free speech protections still apply to the Internet.

Daniel Solove, associate professor at the George Washington University Law School, maintains that an anti-anonymity provision will apply only in cases when the annoyance is part of harassment.

Others argue that Section 113 will not be applied outside of the context of its title: "Preventing Cyberstalking." But those who remember how the Racketeer Influenced and Corrupt Organizations Act (RICO), originally written to target organized crime, was eventually used against pro-life groups in the 'abortion wars' will not be reassured.

## The Future of Section 113

With experts and attorneys already contradicting each other, two things seem clear.

First, we will discover what Section 113 truly means when someone challenges the law. A candidate being mentioned on the Internet is Annoy.com; the site offers a "service by which people send politically incorrect postcards without being required to furnish their identity."

The site owner, Clinton Fein, has a history of "seeking declaratory and injunctive relief" against the Communications Decency Act of 1996 through which "indecent" computer communication that is intended to "annoy" was criminalized. Fein believes Section 113 "warrant[s] a constitutional challenge."

Second, this is a hastily written, bad law that was tacked onto a popular bill. Section 113 may seek to protect against real threats or violence but its language is so vague as to endanger much broader political discussion.

It illustrates why the organization Downsize DC is promoting a "Read the Bills Act," which would require Congressmen to read measures before voting on them.

It is sad that such a commonsense goal sounds utopian.

# Periodical Bibliography

*The following articles have been selected to supplement the diverse views presented in this chapter.*

Fred H. Cate     "Another Notice Isn't Answer," *USA Today*, February 28, 2005.

Jeffrey R. Dion and James A. Ferguson     "Civil Liability for Identity Theft," *Trial*, February 2007.

*Economist*     "A Good Bot Roast; Cyber-Crime," June 23, 2007.

Electronic Frontier Foundation     *RIAA v. The People: Four Years Later*, August 2007. www.eff.org.

*Engineer*     "FOCUS: Crackdown on the Cyber Crooks," April 24, 2006.

Marc Freedman     "Who's Educatin' Who?" *DiaRIAA*, July 23, 2003, www.diariaa.com/essay-mar-education.htm.

Eric Goldman     "The Best and Worse Internet Laws," *InformIT*, April 20, 2007.

Laura Huey and Richard S. Rosenberg     "Watching the Web: Thoughts on Expanding Police Surveillance Opportunities Under the Cyber-Crime Convention," *Canadian Journal of Criminology and Criminal Justice*, October 2004.

Brian Krebs     "Rapid Response Is Best Defense Against ID Theft," *Washington Post*, June 16, 2006.

Thomas M. Lenard and Paul H. Rubin     "Much Ado About Notification," *Regulation*, Spring 2006.

A. Bryan Sartin     "Data Breach Notification Makes Sense—Most of the Time," *CSO Online*, May 1, 2007. www.csoonline.com.

Eric J. Sinrod     "The Erosion of Anonymous Internet Speech," *FindLaw's Writ*, January 27, 2006.

# For Further Discussion

## Chapter 1

1. What commonalities can you find in the rhetoric used by the authors on both sides of the debates in this chapter? Explain, citing from the viewpoints.

2. Chris Swecker claims that identity theft is an increasing problem. Thomas M. Lenard, on the other hand, argues that identity theft is on the decline and that lawmakers should not overreact. Do you think that the authors' affiliations influence their arguments? Explain, citing from the viewpoints.

3. Orrin Hatch and Dave McClure disagree over the impact of Internet piracy on the entertainment industry. Hatch claims it poses a serious threat, while McClure claims the threat is exaggerated. How does each author describe the role of the entertainment industry? Does your answer influence which viewpoint you think is more persuasive? Explain, citing from the viewpoints.

4. Jeff Buckstein maintains that online predators pose a serious threat, especially to young, vulnerable users. Janis Wolak, David Finkelhor, Kimberly J. Mitchell, and Michele L. Ybarra, however, claim that the media hype about online predators is largely inaccurate. Which viewpoint do you find more persuasive? Explain, citing from the viewpoints.

## Chapter 2

1. According to the authors of the viewpoints in this chapter, what are some of the characteristics of the Internet that

make cyber crime possible? Which do you think is the most significant characteristic? Explain, citing from the viewpoints.

2. The authors in this chapter have different ideas about the function and purpose of the Internet. How are these differences reflected in their views on the factors that contribute to cyber crime? Explain, citing from the viewpoints.

3. How do the various factors that the authors in this chapter claim contribute to cyber crime inform the policies that the authors recommend to ameliorate the problem?

4. James Blascovich identifies several fears and insecurities that scam-spammers use to encourage consumers to reveal personal information. To which fears and insecurities do you think you would be most vulnerable? Which fears and insecurities might make your friends, your parents, and your grandparents vulnerable? Explain, providing illustrative details.

# Chapter 3

1. Anita Ramasastry claims that allowing consumers to freeze their credit history is the best way to arm them against identity theft. Stuart Pratt claims that credit freezes do more harm than good. Which viewpoint do you find more persuasive? Explain, citing from the viewpoints.

2. Bruce Schneier maintains that those who develop software should be liable for software flaws. Harris Miller disagrees. What type of evidence does each cite to support his claim? Which type of evidence do you find more persuasive? Explain.

3. Graham Spanier argues that colleges should play a greater role in combating Internet piracy on their campuses. Mark Luker and Michael Petricone claim, on the other hand, that colleges should be spending their time and money on

education. What role do you think colleges should play in combating Internet piracy? Explain, citing from the viewpoints.

4. How do the affiliations of the authors in this chapter influence their rhetoric? What type of rhetoric do you find most persuasive? Explain, citing from the viewpoints.

## Chapter 4

1. What commonalities can you find in the rhetoric used by the authors in both sides of the debate over what laws will be prevent cyber crime? Which strategies do you think are most persuasive? Explain, citing from the viewpoints.

2. The Cyber Security Industry Alliance (CSIA) asserts that the Cybercrime Treaty will help the worldwide fight against cyber crime. Bob Barr fears that the treaty will threaten U.S. sovereignty and security. Do you think that the CSIA adequately addresses Barr's concerns? Explain, citing from the viewpoints.

3. Mitch Bainwol and Cary Sherman argue that suing students is necessary to combat Internet piracy. Fred von Lohmann claims that suing students will not reduce Internet piracy. How do the authors' affiliations influence their rhetoric? Which viewpoint do you find more persuasive? Explain.

4. Jim McDermott and Wendy McElroy disagree concerning the effectiveness of a federal cyber-stalking law. What rhetorical strategy does each author use to support his or her claim? Which strategy do you find more persuasive? Explain, citing from the viewpoints.

# Organizations to Contact

*The editors have compiled the following list of organizations concerned with the issues debated in this book. The descriptions are derived from materials provided by the organizations. All have publications or information available for interested readers. The list was compiled on the date of publication of the present volume; the information provided here may change. Be aware that many organizations take several weeks or longer to respond to inquiries, so allow as much time as possible.*

**American Civil Liberties Union (ACLU)**
125 Broad Street, 18th Floor, New York, NY   10004
Web site: www.aclu.org

The American Civil Liberties Union (ACLU) works to uphold civil rights, focusing specifically on rights such as free speech, equal protection, due process, and privacy. The ACLU takes court cases that address and whose rulings define these civil liberties; in recent years, many ACLU court cases have addressed issues such as Internet censorship and library Web blocking. Reports on Internet censorship such as the "Fact Sheet on Children's Internet Protection Act," and "Censorship in a Box: Why Blocking Software is Wrong for Public Libraries," are available on the ACLU Web site.

**Berkman Center for Internet and Society**
23 Everett Street, 2nd Floor, Cambridge, MA   02138
(617) 495-7547 • fax: (617) 495-7641
e-mail: cyber@law.harvard.edu
Web site: http://cyber.law.harvard.edu

The Berkman Center for Internet and Society conducts research on legal, technical, and social developments in cyberspace and assesses the need or lack thereof for laws and sanctions. It publishes a monthly newsletter, *The Filter*, blog posts, and articles based on the center's research efforts, many of which are available on its Web site, including "Overcoming the Achilles Heel of Copyright Law" and "Why Youth ♡ Social Network Sites: The Role of Networked Publics in Teenage Social Life."

## Cato Institute

1000 Massachusetts Avenue NW
Washington, DC 20001-5403
(202) 842-0200 • fax: (202) 842-3490
e-mail: cato@cato.org
Web site: www.cato.org

The Cato Institute is a libertarian public policy research foundation that aims to limit the role of government and protect civil liberties. The institute publishes the quarterlies, *CATO Journal* and *Regulation*, and the bimonthly *Cato Policy Report*. Its Web site publishes selections from these and other publications, including "Much Ado About Notification," "Digging Piracy," and "Government Can't Protect Kids from Porn—But Parents Can."

## Center for Democracy and Technology (CDT)

1634 Eye Street NW, #1100, Washington, DC 20006
(202) 637-9800 • fax: (202) 637-0968
Web site: www.cdt.org

The Center for Democracy and Technology (CDT) works to ensure that regulations concerning all current and emerging forms of technology are in accordance with democratic values, especially free expression and privacy. CDT works to promote its ideals through research and education as well as grassroots movements. On its Web site, CDT publishes articles papers, reports, and testimony, including "Privacy and Identity Management," "MySpace: Coming of Age for Coming of Age," and "The Internet at Risk: The Need for Higher Education Advocacy."

## Center for Safe and Responsible Internet Use (CSRIU)

474 W. Twenty-Ninth Avenue, Eugene, OR    97405

(541) 344-9125 • fax: (541) 344-1481

e-mail: info@csriu.org

Web site: http://cyberbully.org

The Center for Safe and Responsible Internet Use (CSRIU) is dedicated to educating parents, educators, and policy makers about the most effective methods of encouraging safe and responsible Internet use by children and teens. CSRIU emphasizes the importance of equipping youth with the knowledge and personal strength to make good decisions that will keep them out of potentially harmful situations when using the Internet. Copies of reports by CSRIU executive director Nancy Willard, such as "I Can't See You—You Can't See Me," "A Briefing for Educators: Online Social Networking Communities and Youth Risk," and "Cyber-Safe Kids, Cyber-Savvy Teens" are available on its Web site.

## Consumer Data Industry Association (CDIA)

1090 Vermont Avenue NW, Washington, DC    20005

(202) 371-0910 • fax: (202) 371-0134

e-mail: cdia@cdiaonline.org

Web site: www.cdiaonline.org

The Consumer Data Industry Association (CDIA) is an international trade association of consumer information companies that provide fraud prevention and risk management products, credit and mortgage reports, tenant and employment screening services, check fraud and verification services, and collection services. The association lobbies on behalf of the consumer information industry before state and federal legislators. It also sets industry standards and provides business and professional education. CDIA provides consumer education materials on consumer credit rights and credit reporting, some of which are available on its Web site.

**Electronic Frontier Foundation (EFF)**
454 Shotwell Street, San Francisco, CA 94110-1914
(415) 436-9333 • fax: (415) 436-9993
e-mail: information@eff.org
Web site: www.eff.org

The Electronic Frontier Foundation (EFF) is an organization that aims to promote a better understanding of telecommunications issues. It fosters awareness of civil liberties issues arising from advancements in computer-based communications media, and supports litigation to preserve, protect, and extend First Amendment rights in computing and telecommunications technologies. EFF's publications include *Building the Open Road, Crime and Puzzlement,* the quarterly newsletter *Networks & Policy,* the biweekly electronic newsletter *EFFector Online,* and white papers and articles, including "A Better Way Forward: Voluntary Collective Licensing of Music File Sharing" and "Back to School for Reading, Writing, and RIAA Lawsuits?"

**Federal Trade Commission (FTC) Consumer Response Center**
600 Pennsylvania Avenue, NW, Washington, DC 20580
(202) 326-2222
Web site: www.ftc.gov/bcp/edu/microsites/idtheft

The FTC Identify Theft Web site, Deter, Detect, Defend—Avoid ID Theft, is a resource for consumers, businesses, and law enforcement to learn about the crime of identity theft. On the Web site, consumers can learn how to avoid identity theft and what to do if their identity is stolen, businesses can learn how to prevent problems and help their customers deal with identity theft, and law enforcement can find resources to help victims of identity theft. Articles available on its Web site include "ID Theft: What It's All About" and "Privacy Choices for Your Personal Financial Information." The Web site Reference Desk provides link to laws, reports, and testimony on identity theft issues.

## Free Expression Policy Project (FEPP)
170 W. Seventy-Sixth Street, #301, New York, NY   10023
e-mail: margeheins@verizon.net
Web site: www.fepproject.org

Founded in 2000, Free Expression Policy Project (FEPP) is a research and advocacy organization working to ensure first amendment rights with regard to Internet restrictions, copyright laws, youth censorship, and more. The organization publishes policy reports and fact sheets such as *Internet Filters* and *Sex and Censorship*, which are available on its Web site. In addition, the Web site posts commentaries on the project's issues, including "Understanding *Grokster*" and "Do You Own What Is Yours? The Case of Promotional CDs."

## Identity Theft Resource Center (ITRC)
PO Box 26822, San Diego, CA   92196
(858) 693-7935
e-mail: itrc@idtheftcenter.org
Web site: www.idtheftcenter.org

The Identity Theft Resource Center (ITRC) serves as an information for identify-theft victims. The Web site publishes templates for letters to companies and bill collectors. Its Web site reference library also includes articles on identity theft, including the ITRC founder's own story.

## Pew Internet and American Life Project
1615 L Street NW, Suite 700, Washington, DC   20036
(202) 419-4500 • fax: (202) 419-4505
Web site: www.pewinternet.org

The Pew Internet Project is an initiative of the Pew Research Center. The project explores the impact of the Internet on children, families, communities, the workplace, schools, health care, and civic/political life. Pew Internet provides data and analysis on Internet usage and its effects on American society. On its Web site, the project provides access to articles and reports, including "Music Downloading and Listening: Findings from the Pew Internet and American Life Project," "Teens and Social Media," and "Privacy Implications of Fast, Mobile Internet Access."

## Progress and Freedom Foundation (PFF)

1444 I Street NW, Suite 500, Washington, DC   20005
(202) 289-8928 • fax: (202) 289-6079
e-mail: mail@pff.org
Web site: www.pff.org

Progress and Freedom Foundation (PFF) is a think tank that studies public policy related to the Internet. Its mission is to educate policy makers, opinion leaders, and the public about issues associated with technological change, based on a philosophy of limited government, free markets, and individual sovereignty. The foundation publishes the newsletter, *PFF Flash*. On its Web site, the foundation provides access to articles by PFF experts, including "A Performance Right for Recording Artists: Sound Policy at Home and Abroad," "Stepping on the Toes of Giants: What Not to Think About Copyright," and "Net Neutrality: A Fairness Doctrine for the Internet."

## Recording Industry Association of America (RIAA)

1025 F Street NW, 10th Floor, Washington, DC   20004
(202) 775-0101
Web site: www.riaa.com

Recording Industry Association of America (RIAA) is a trade group that represents the U.S. recording industry. Its mission is to foster a business and legal climate that supports and promotes its members' creative and financial vitality. RIAA works to protect intellectual property rights worldwide and the First Amendment rights of artists. It conducts consumer, industry, and technical research and monitors and reviews state and federal laws, regulations, and policies. On its Web site, RIAA publishes fact sheets on key recording industry issues, including "Piracy: Online and on the Street" and "Top 5 Reasons to Not Download Illegally."

**WiredSafety**
96 Linwood Plaza, #417, Ft. Lee, NJ   07024-3701
(201) 463-8663
e-mail: askparry@wiredsafety.org
Web site: www.wiredsafety.org

Operating online since 1995, WiredSafety is an Internet patrol organization that not only monitors the Web for safety violations, but also provides education on all aspects of Internet safety. Volunteers worldwide offer their time and are the driving force of the organization. The WiredSafety Web site provides information categorized and specialized for parents, educators, law enforcement, and youth; additionally, topical issues such as social networks, cyber-bullying, and cyber-dating are discussed. Links to issue and age specific projects such as Teenangels, WiredKids, StopCyberbullying, and Internet Super Heroes are available on the Web site as well.

# Bibliography of Books

Pamela Donovan   *No Way of Knowing: Crime, Urban Legends, and the Internet.* New York: Routledge, 2004.

Johan Eriksson and Glampiero Giacomello, eds.   *International Relations and Security in the Digital Age.* New York: Routledge, 2007.

William W. Fisher   *Promises to Keep: Technology, Law, and the Future of Entertainment.* Stanford, CA: Stanford University Press, 2004.

Jack Goldsmith and Timothy Wu   *Who Controls the Internet? Illusions of a Borderless World.* New York: Oxford University Press, 2006.

Seymour E. Goodman and Herbert S. Lin, eds.   *Toward a Safer and More Secure Cyberspace.* Washington, DC: National Academies Press, 2007.

Yvonne Jewkes, ed.   *Dot.cons: Crime, Deviance and Identity on the Internet.* Cullompton, UK: Willan, 2002.

Joseph Migga Kizza and Florence M. Kizza   *Securing the Information Infrastructure.* Hershey, PA: Cybertech, 2008.

Robin M. Kowalski, Susan P. Limber and Patricia W. Agatston   *Cyber Bullying: Bullying in the Digital Age.* Oxford, UK: Blackwell, 2008.

Lawrence Lessig — *Free Culture: How Big Media Uses Technology and the Law to Lock Down Culture and Control Creativity.* New York: Penguin, 2004.

James A. Lewis, ed. — *Cyber Security: Turning National Solutions into International Cooperation.* Washington, DC: Center for Strategic and International Studies Press, 2003.

Martin C. Libicki — *Conquest in Cyberspace: National Security and Information Warfare.* New York: Cambridge University Press, 2007.

David A. May and James E. Headley — *Identity Theft.* New York: P. Lang, 2004.

Kevin D. Mitnik — *The Art of Intrusion: The Real Stories Behind the Exploits of Hackers, Intruders & Deceivers.* Hoboken, NJ: Wiley Publishing, 2005.

Robert O'Harrow — *No Place to Hide.* New York: Free Press, 2005.

Aernout Schmidt, Wilfred Dolfsma, Wim Keuvelaar — *Fighting the War on File Sharing.* The Hague, Netherlands: T.M.C. Asser Press, distributed by Cambridge University Press, 2007.

Julian Sher — *Caught in the Web: Inside the Police Hunt to Rescue Children from Online Predators.* New York: Carroll & Graf, 2007.

Daniel J. Solove — *The Digital Person: Technology and Privacy in the Information Age.* New York: New York University Press, 2004.

Daniel J. Solove — *The Future of Reputation: Gossip, Rumor, and Privacy on the Internet.* New Haven, CT: Yale University Press, 2007.

Michael Strangelove — *The Empire of Mind: Digital Piracy and the Anti-Capitalist Movement.* Toronto, Ontario, Canada: University of Toronto Press, 2005.

Bob Sullivan — *Your Evil Twin: Behind the Identity Theft Epidemic.* Hoboken, NJ: Wiley Publishing, 2004.

Adam Thierer and Wayne Crews, eds. — *Who Rules the Net? A New Guide to Navigating the Proposed Rules of the Road for Cyberspace.* Washington, DC: Cato Institute, 2003.

Wally Wang — *Steal This File Sharing Book: What They Won't Tell You About File Sharing.* San Francisco, CA: No Starch, 2004.

Nancy E. Willard — *Cyberbullying and Cyberthreats: Responding to the Challenge of Online Social Aggression, Threats, and Distress.* Champaign, IL: Research Press, 2007.

# Index

## A

Abduction, 63, 66, 70, 71–72
Abrams, Martin, 113
Academic community, and piracy,
  131–134, 135–139, 166–172, 173–
  176
Address changes, identity theft
  tool, 24
Afghanistan, 96, 100–102
Aftab, Parry, 107, 143
Ages, sex crime victims, 63, 69,
  70–71
Air gapping, 37, 44, 45
Air traffic control system, 45
Airliner security, 44–45
American Civil Liberties Union
  (ACLU), 164
Annoy.com, 186
Applications, credit, 121–122
ARPANET, 15
Artists
  Internet use, 59
  rights, 92, 93, 175
ATMs, 38
Atta, Mohamed, 96
Aubuchon, Gary, 142
Automatic uploading, 53–54

## B

Bailey, Kirk, 179
Bainwol, Mitch, 166–172
Balkam, Stephen, 66
Banks, 25, 38
Barr, Bob, 162–165
Betamax-Sony case, 55–56

Biological weapons, 97–98
Bishop, Todd, 129
Black hat hackers, 79
Blocking of file sharing. *See* Net-
  work anti-sharing technologies
Blunt, Matt, 142
Bootleg merchandise, 54
Boyd, Danah, 20, 143
Breaches
  ChoicePoint, 115, 152
  Citigroup, 152
  definition altered by lobbyists,
    153–154
  federal notification laws won't
    protect consumers, 150–155
  federal notification standard is
    necessary, 144–149
  LexisNexis, 152
  manufacturers' liability, 123–
    126, 127–130
  most caused by insiders,
    81–85
  notification following, 31–32,
    149, 151–152
  victims sampling, 85
Brick-and-mortar music stores,
  168
Buckstein, Jeff, 62–67
Bush, George W., 36
  Sec. 113, Violence Against
    Women Act, 181, 183, 184
  support of Cybercrime Treaty,
    163, 164, 165
  terrorism pronouncements,
    41–42
Business Software Alliance, 171

# C

California
breach disclosure law (SB1386), 31, 146–147, 151, 152
security freeze laws, 117
Carosella, John, 19–20
Cassell, Justine, 20
CDs, 93, 138, 175
CEA (Consumer Electronics Association), 138
Center for Information Policy Leadership, 113
cGrid, 171
Chat rooms
growing use, 74
stalker use, 179
terrorist use, 97
Cheney, Dick, 41–42
Child molesters. *See* Internet predators
Child pornography, 64, 72–75
programs, finding perpetrators, 87–88
youth-posted, 65, 73
ChoicePoint (data broker), 115, 152
Citigroup, 152
Civil liberties
cybercrime treaty threatens, 162–165
RIAA threat, 92
Civil unrest, 93–94
Clarke, Richard, 42
Codes
hacking, 79
security, 44
Coll, Steve, 95–103
Collaborative learning, 132

Colleges
anti-sharing technologies costly and ineffective, 137, 174
should not be forced to fight piracy, 135–139, 174–176
should play greater role fighting piracy, 131–134, 166, 167, 171–172
*See also* Intellectual property; Students
Communications Act of 1934, 183
Communications Decency Act of 1996, 186
Communities
social networking, 19, 20
terrorist, 99–100, 103
Compact discs, 93, 138, 175
Competition, information sector, 32–33
Congress
active litigation and, 55
Cybercrime Treaty and, 165
cyberstalking laws and, 178, 180–181, 183
file-sharing cases and, 55, 169, 174
Consumer Electronics Association (CEA), 138
Consumer protection
consumer permission, 112
consumer preauthorization, 113
lacking, online merchants, 16–17
Contract employees, 82
Control systems, 39
Convention on Cybercrime
improves fight against Internet crime, 156–161

ratification, 160–161
treaty threatens civil liberties, 162–165
U.S. contribution, 158–160
Copyright
dual nature, 138
unnecessary penalties, 60
Copyright infringement. *See* File sharing; Piracy
CopySense, 172
Costs
employee monitoring, 84–85
losses, Internet crime, 17, 23, 31, 43, 117, 118
losses, piracy, 59, 167, 168
notification, 31–32, 151–153
software lawsuits, 129
Council of Europe, Convention on Cybercrime, 157–161, 162–165
Credit applications, 121–122
Credit bureaus, 117–118
Credit card companies, 16, 31, 112
card issuing costs, 153
counter cardholder freeze ability, 118
grant easy credit, 116, 154
Credit card fraud
costs, 31
methods, 16–17, 24, 25
not part of identity theft, 23, 32
Credit histories
consumers should be able to freeze, 114–119
consumers should not be able to freeze, 120–122
Credit market, 112–113, 115, 116, 151
Credit ratings, 27, 116

Criminal organizations, 22
Customer lists, 33, 112
Cyber-bullying (Meier case), 65–67, 142–143
Cyber Division, FBI, 23, 42
Cyber Security Industry Alliance, 156–161
Cybercrime Treaty. *See* Convention on Cybercrime
Cybersecurity, 43–46, 147
*See also* Data security
Cyberstalking, 104–109
federal law threatens free speech, 182–187
federal law will protect victims, 177–181
Cyberterrorism, 99
experiment games, 45, 48
media coverage, 42
problem is exaggerated, 40–50
serious threat to global security, 35–39

**D**

Danger, real life, 19–20
DARPA (Defense Department's Advanced Research Projects Agency), 14–15
Data Accountability and Trust Act (DATA), 153–154
Data brokerage, 112–113, 115, 151
Data security, 29–30
definitions weakened, 153–154
privacy and, 28, 32–33
software, 79–80
vulnerable to insiders, 81–85
*See also* Breaches; Cybersecurity
de Fontenay, Eric, 91

Dead drops, translated to Web, 102

Defense Department's Advanced Research Projects Agency (DARPA), 14–15

Denning, Dorothy, 43, 45

Department of Justice, 79, 105, 159, 164

Developers, software, 124, 126

Digital Freedom Campaign, 138

Digital Millennium Copyright Act (DMCA), 92

Digital revolution, 27, 60–61

Disclosure, breach. *See* Notification, breach/fraud

Dorgan, Byron, 113

Drug abuse, 72

Dumpster diving, 24

**E**

E-commerce, 15, 16

E-mail
 abusive, 82, 105, 108, 178, 179
 history, 19
 terrorist use, 48, 102–103

Easy credit, 116, 154

EDUCAUSE, 136–137, 138

Electronic Frontier Foundation, 175

Electronic Privacy Information Center, 137

Employees
 contract, 82
 disgruntled, 84
 security opinions, 147
 security risks, 47, 48, 81–85

Encryption, 39, 98, 103

Entertainment industry
 internet piracy threatens, 51–56

overstates problem of internet piracy, 57–61

Estonia, 36

Europe
 Council of, and Cybercrime Treaty, 157–161
 identity theft, 113

"Evans, Josh," 66

Exhibitionism, online, 65, 73

**F**

FAA (Federal Aviation Administration), 45

Fair Credit Reporting Act of 1970, 112, 121

Fair use, 138

False identities
 illegality, Violence Against Women Act, 183–184, 185, 186
 part of predator stereotype, 69
 social networking, 66, 142

Family Online Safety Institute, 66

FBI. *See* Federal Bureau of Investigation (FBI)

Fear
 cyberterrorism, 41–43, 49–50
 Internet, 15

Federal Aviation Administration (FAA), 45

Federal Bureau of Investigation (FBI)
 Cyber Division, 23, 42
 identity theft, 22
 joint initiatives, 23–25
 sexual predator cases, 63

Federal laws
 data breach notification, 147–149, 153–155

financial, health industries, 148

weak, preempting strong state laws, 151, 154

Federal Trade Commission (FTC)

identity theft warnings, 24, 115–116

identity theft work, 17, 23, 25

penalties, 115

Fein, Clinton, 186

File sharing

crackdown on students is ineffective, 173–176

crackdown on students is necessary, 131–134, 166–172

increase, despite lawsuits, 92–94, 136, 175

network blocking technologies, 137, 169, 171–172, 174

peer-to-peer is rebellion against tyranny, 91–94

user numbers, 93, 168

See also Piracy

File-sharing networks (piracy rings), 52–53, 55, 58

File-sharing software, 53–55

See also Network anti-sharing technologies; specific sites

Financial institution impersonation, 24

Finch, Simon, 35–39

Finkelhor, David, 68–76

Fraud, identity. See Identity theft

Free speech, endangered, 184–187

Freedman, Marc, 91–94

Freedom and Innovation Revitalizing U.S. Entrepreneurship Act of 2007, 138

Freezing, credit histories

should be an option, 114–119

should not be an option, 120–122

FTC (Federal Trade Commission). See Federal Trade Commission (FTC)

G

Garbage, identity theft tool, 24

Glasser, Susan B., 95–103

Glickman, Dan, 136, 137

Global Islamic Media Front, 101

Gohring, Nancy, 86–90

Government Information systems, 41–46, 49–50

Gramm-Leach-Bliley (GBL) law, 148

Gray hat hackers, 79

Green, Joshua, 40–50

Grokster, 55, 136

Grokster, MGM v. (2005), 173

H

Hackers

identity theft contributions, 25

methods, 17

motivations, 47, 79, 88

police dealings, 89

unfairly blamed, 81–85

vigilantism, and consequences, 86–90

Hackett, Emily, 15, 16

Hahn, Robert, 112

Hanssen, Robert, 47

Harassment, 184–185

See also Cyber-bullying; Cyberstalking

Hasan, Ragib, 144–149

Hatch, Orrin, 51–56

Helpfulness, hackers, 79
Higher education. *See* Colleges
HIPAA law, 148
Hitchcock, Jayne, 106, 107
Hollywood, piracy complaints, 57, 58–61, 136
HR3997 (federal disclosure law proposal), 154
Hutton, Thomas, 143

**I**

iDefense, 43–44
Identifying information, personal, 146
   economic value, 28–29, 34, 112–113, 154
   misleading definition, lobbyists', 153
   *See also* False identities; Identity theft; Notification, breach/fraud
Identity theft
   data brokerage and, 112–113, 115, 153–154
   is a declining problem, 26–34
   is a serious problem, 21–25, 115–116, 151
   offline occurrences, 16, 24, 32
   preventing, via credit freeze, 116–118, 122
   scope, 22–23, 24
   trigger events, 148–149
Iger, Bob, 136
Inducing Infringement of Copyrights Act (Hatch/Leahy), 56
Information economy, 27, 32–33, 34
Information technology (IT) employees, 81, 82, 84–85

Infrastructure targets, 46, 47–48, 49
Innovation
   copyright and, 138
   regulation may hamper, 28
Inside jobs, 47, 48, 81–85
Instant messaging, 64, 69, 74
Intellectual property, 131–133, 138, 168–169, 171
Intelligence agency security, 45–46
   *See also* Federal Bureau of Investigation (FBI)
International aspects, cybercrime, 156–161, 162–165
Internet
   disruptive technology, 27, 60–61
   enabling stalkers, 104–109, 177–181
   free speech issues, 184–187
   global policing, 156–161
   helps promote terrorism, 95–103
   history, 14–15, 19
   university-provided services, 132–133, 136–137, 172, 176
Internet advertising, 33
Internet Alliance, 15
Internet Crime Complaint Center (IC3), 17, 24–25
Internet Crime Report, 17
Internet predators
   criminal histories, 72–73
   differ from pedophiles, 70–71
   media stereotype is inaccurate, 68–76
   nonviolent, 71–72
   punishment, 74
   serious threat, 62–67, 177–181

Internet Service Providers (ISPs), 164, 168
iPods, 82, 176
Iraq, 96, 97, 100

**J**

Jihadists. *See* al-Qaeda; Terrorism
Joint Committee of the Higher Education and Entertainment Communities, 169
Joint initiatives, law enforcement/ FBI, 23–25
Justice Department, 79, 105, 159, 164

**K**

Kazaa, 53, 55, 58
Keong, Victor, 79–80
Kerr, Kenneth, 15
Kerr, Orin, 185–186
Kline, Ronald, 89, 90
Kozakiewicz, Alicia, 63, 66

**L**

bin Laden, Osama, 98, 100–101, 103
Law enforcement
cyberstalking, 107–108, 179
global, cybercrime, 157–161, 163–164
hacker crackdowns, 89–90
joint initiatives, FBI, 23–25
Laws
credit security freezes, 117– 119, 121, 122
cyber-bullying, 142–143
cyberstalking, 108, 177–181, 182–187

federal, breach notification, 147–149, 153–155
state, breach notification, 145– 147, 151
Lawsuits
file sharing, general public, 92, 94
file sharing, students/colleges, 136, 137–138, 139, 167, 169– 170, 174–175
file sharing and secondary liability, 54–56
software breaches, 126, 128– 130
Leahy, Patrick, 56
Lenard, Thomas M., 26–34
Levine, D.E., 99
LexisNexis, 152
Liability, credit card theft, 16, 116
Libicki, Martin, 44, 45, 47, 49
Ligon, Joelle, 178–181
Lobbyists against data theft notification, 152, 153–154
Losses, business. *See* Costs
Lucas, George, 58
Luker, Mark, 135–139

**M**

Madden, Mary, 59
Mail theft, 24, 25
Market failures, 28–29
Marketing, 29, 113, 125
McClure, Dave, 57–61
McCullagh, Declan, 164, 183–184
McDermott, Jim, 177–181
McElroy, Wendy, 182–187
Media Awareness Network (Canada), 65
Media portrayals, 42, 43, 44

Meier, Megan, 65–66, 142–143

Member States, European Union, 157–158, 160

Message boards, 97, 102, 106

*MGM v. Grokster* (2005), 173

MI5, 37

Microsoft, 80, 129

Mierzwinski, Edward, 16

Military, U.S., 37, 43–44

Millennium Bug, 36

Miller, Harris, 127–130

Min, Gary, 83

Mir, Hamid, 96

Mismanagement, data, 81–85

Mitchell, Kimberly J., 68–76

Mobility, and data vulnerability, 83

Mohamed, Khalid Sheik, 102–103

Moles, 47

Monitoring

    breach-seeking, 137, 149

    educational institutions, 137

    home pc software, 66

Monopolies, software, 125

Motion Picture Association of America (MPAA), 133, 136

Murder, 71

Music artists. *See* Artists

MySpace, 142

**N**

N-JOV (National Juvenile Online Victimization) Study, 69, 71, 72, 73

Napster, 93, 176

Nasar, Mustafa Setmariam, 97–98

National Center for Missing and Exploited Children (NCMEC), 64–65

National Child Exploitation Coordination Centre, 65

National Crime Victimization Survey, 75

National School Boards Association, 143

Network anti-sharing technologies, 137, 169, 171–172, 174

Neuburger, Jeff, 89–90

New account frauds, 23

*New Hampshire, Sweezy v.* (1957), 137

Notification, breach/fraud, 31–32, 145, 151–152

    federal standard is necessary, 144–149

    pertinent information, 149

    weak federal laws won't protect consumers, 150–155

Nuclear weapons, 37, 41, 42, 43, 44

**O**

Online predators. *See* Internet predators

Opting out/in, 113

Outwater, Meredith, 17

**P**

P2P. *See* File sharing

Packets, 14, 15

Paranoia, 45–46

Parental monitoring, 66

Patches, software, 79–80, 124

Pedophiles, 68, 70–71, 72–76

Peer-to-peer file sharing. *See* File sharing

Penn State, 131, 132, 133

Permission, consumer, 112–113

Personal information. *See* Identifying information, personal

Petricone, Michael, 135–139

Phishing, 24, 83

Physical communication, 19–20, 98

Physical targets. *See* Infrastructure targets

PINs (personal identification numbers), 119, 122

Piracy

anti-sharing technologies, 137, 169, 171–172, 174

colleges have no obligation to fight, 135–139

colleges should play greater role fighting, 131–134, 166, 167, 171–172

consequences, 52

problem is overstated, 57–61

threatens entertainment industry, 51–56

*See also* File sharing

Piracy rings, 52–53, 55, 58

PIRG (U.S. Public Interest Research Group), 16

Politicians' worries, cyber-terror, 36–37

Pornography

child, 64, 72–75

programs, finding perpetrators, 87–88

self-posted, 65, 73

Pratt, Stuart, 120–122

Predators. *See* Internet predators

Pregnancy, teen, 75

Privacy, 34

advocates, 116, 148

consumer expectations, 29

data security and, 28, 31–33, 148

loss, due to Cybercrime Treaty, 163–165

*See also* Notification, breach/fraud

Private sector security, 43–44

Pseudonyms, online, 66, 184

Publishing, Internet, and free speech, 184–186

**Q**

al-Qaeda

internet usage and planning, 48–49, 96–98, 100–103

plots/speculation, 37, 42, 46

*See also* Cyberterrorism; Terrorism

**R**

Racketeer Influenced and Corrupt Organizations Act (RICO), 186

Radford, Benjamin, 74

Ramasastry, Anita, 114–119

Rape, 69, 71

RCMP (Royal Canadian Mounted Police), 65

Read the Bills Act, 187

The Real IRA, 37

Record stores, 168

Recording industry, power, 52, 93, 94

Recording Industry Association of America (RIAA)

failed campaign, 175

file-sharers' opinions, 91–93, 94

lawsuits, students/colleges, 137–138, 139, 167, 169–170, 174–175
Registry, sex offenders, 74
Regulation concerns, 27–28, 32–34, 128
Rehman, Waqas "Michael," 64
Reid, John, 36
Remote access
corporate attacks, 84
nonexistent, airlines, 45
nonexistent, nuclear weapons, 44
personal pcs, 87–88
SCADA systems, 46
Reputation, businesses, 29
Rhapsody, 176
RIAA (Recording Industry Association of America). *See* Recording Industry Association of America (RIAA)
Ridge, Tom, 41
Royal Canadian Mounted Police (RCMP), 65
Royalties, music artists, 175–176
Ruckus, 172
Runaways, 71

**S**

Sanford, Hurt, 113
Sartin, A. Bryan, 152
SCADA systems, 46, 47
Scheuer, Michael, 98
Schmidt, Howard, 124, 126
Schneier, Bruce, 88, 112–113, 123–126, 150–155
Schools. *See* Colleges
Schumer, Charles, 45, 49
Scripts, hacking, 79
Secondary liability, 55–56

Secret communications, 102–103
Security
codes, 44
corporate, 81–85
experts, 79–80, 82, 83, 84, 85
software, 79–80, 123–126, 127–130
Self-posted pornography, 65, 73
September 11, 2001 attacks
increasing cyberterrorism discussion, 41–42
manual nature, 45
Sex crime rates, 75–76
Sexual predation
media stereotypes are inaccurate, 68–76
online danger, 19, 20, 62–67
Sharman Networks, 55
Shehan, John, 64
Sherman, Cary, 134, 166–172
Sichelman, Lew, 122
Silverstein, Kacy, 104–109
Simulation games, 45, 48
Sinrod, Eric J., 185
Skimming, 24
Social music sharing (physical), 138
Social networking sites, 20, 143
Social Security numbers, 22, 112, 115, 146, 153
Socializing. *See* Chat rooms; Social networking sites
Software, monitoring, 66
Software security, 79–80, 124–125
manufacturers should be liable for breaches, 123–126
manufacturers should not be liable for breaches, 127–130

Sony-Betamax case (*Sony Corp v. Universal City Studios,* 1984), 55–56

Spam, 24, 25, 102–103

Spanier, Graham, 131–134

Stalkers

combating, 108–109, 177, 179–181

motivations, 105, 107, 180

pursuing victims via Internet, 104–109, 177–181

Stansell-Gamm, Martha, 79

State laws

cyberstalking/harassment, 143

data breach notification, 145–147, 151

federal preemption, 151, 154

State regulation, 33–34, 119

Statutory rape, 69

Stereotypes, Internet predators, 68–70

Sting operations, 70, 72

Straus, Eric, 20

Straw, Jack, 36

Students

crackdown on copyright infringers is necessary, 131–134, 166–172

crackdown on file sharing is ineffective, 173–176

disciplinary action, 172, 174

*See also* Colleges

Substance abuse, 72

Suicide, 65–66, 142–143

Supervisory control and data acquisition systems, 46, 47

Swecker, Chris, 21–25

*Sweezy v. New Hampshire* (1957), 137

Swihart, Jonathan, 93

Swire, Peter, 49–50

**T**

Taliban, 96, 100

Technological shifts, 27, 60–61

Teen pregnancy rates, 75

Telecommunications Act of 1996, 179, 186

Telephone fraud, 25

Terrorism

communities, 99–100, 103

facilitated on Internet, 95–103

Internet recruitment, 97

Internet training, 96–98, 101–102

vs. cyberterrorism, 41–43, 45, 99

*See also* al-Qaeda

Terrorism Research Center, 101, 102

Theft, physical, 15, 16, 24, 25

Third-party vendors, 82, 83–84, 125

*To Catch a Predator* (television program), 70

Totalitarianism, 92

Trade secrets, 83

Trafficking of files. *See* File sharing

Trash, identity theft tool, 24

Treaty, Cybercrime

threatens civil liberties, 162–165

will improve global fight on Internet crime, 156–161

Trojan horse programs, 87–90

Tyree, Scott, 63

# U

Ugwu, Eberechi P., 38
Unconscious uploading, and piracy, 53–54
Undercover work, 37, 70, 72, 86–90
United Kingdom, threats, 36, 37
*Universal City Studios, Sony Corp v.* (1984), 55–56
Universities. *See* Colleges
Uploading, media files, 52–54
U.S. Public Interest Research Group (PIRG), 16

# V

Vasquez, Daniel, 64
Victims
    identity theft, 16, 23, 30–31, 115–119, 151
    stalking, 106–107, 108–109, 177–181
Video production, terrorist, 101
Vigilante justice, 86–90, 88
Violence
    Internet predators' low rates, 71–72
    against women, 105, 106, 109, 177–181, 182–187
Violence Against Women Act (Sec. 113)
    approval, 181, 183
    threatens free speech, 182–187
Viruses
    network infection, 37
    worms, 128, 130, 158
Volokh, Eugene, 184
Voluntary standards, 29
von Lohmann, Fred, 173–176
Vulnerabilities, software, 79–80

# W

Wagner, Breanne, 45
*WarGames* (film), 42, 44
Warren, Earl, 137
Washkuch, Frank Jr., 81–85
Watchdog groups, 89, 90
Weapons of mass destruction
    cyberterrorism compared, 41–43
    nuclear, 37, 41, 42, 43, 44
    terrorist training, 97–98
Web cameras, 72, 73, 74
Web sites
    defacement, 47
    terrorist, 98–99, 102
Webcams, 65
Weimann, Gabriel, 98–99
White-collar crime, 23
White hat hackers, 79
Willman, Brad, 87–90
Wireless networks, 44, 74
Wizards, 53
Wolak, Janis, 68–76
Working to Halt Online Abuse (WHOA), 106
Worms. *See* Viruses

# Y

Ybarra, Michelle L., 68–76
YISS-2 (Youth Internet Safety Survey 2), 73
Y2K Bug, 36
Yurcik, William, 144–149

# Z

Zawahiri, Ayman, 101